HANDBOOK OF NATURE STUDY:

MAMMALS, FLOWERLESS PLANTS

COMPLETE YOUR COLLECTION TODAY!

ANNA COMSTOCK'S
HANDBOOK OF NATURE-STUDY

Reptiles, Amphibians, Fish and Invertebrates

ANNA COMSTOCK'S
HANDBOOK OF NATURE-STUDY

Birds

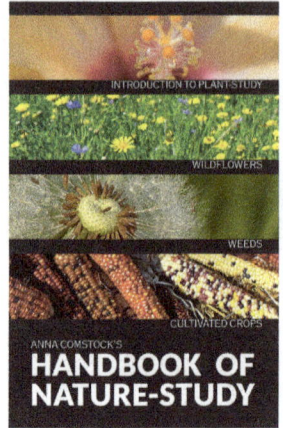

ANNA COMSTOCK'S
HANDBOOK OF NATURE-STUDY

Wildflowers, Weeds and Cultivated Crops

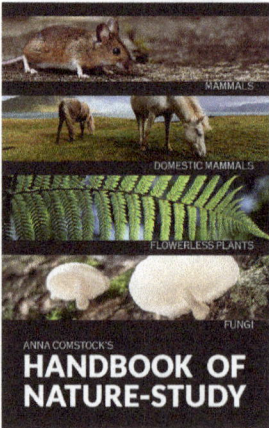

ANNA COMSTOCK'S
HANDBOOK OF NATURE-STUDY

Mammals and Flowerless Plants

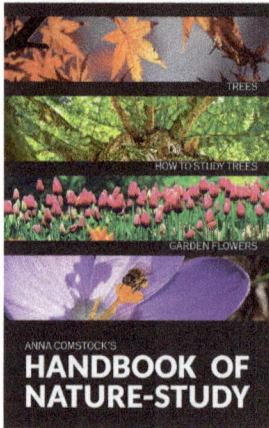

ANNA COMSTOCK'S
HANDBOOK OF NATURE-STUDY

Trees and Garden Flowers

ANNA COMSTOCK'S
HANDBOOK OF NATURE-STUDY

Earth and Sky

ANNA COMSTOCK'S
HANDBOOK OF NATURE-STUDY

Insects

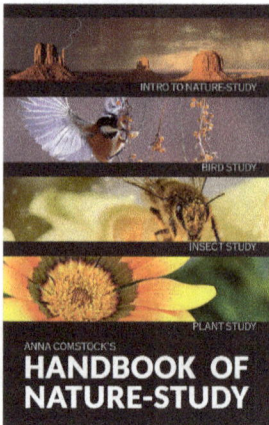

ANNA COMSTOCK'S
HANDBOOK OF NATURE-STUDY

Introduction

Available at all
online book retailers

LIVING BOOK
PRESS

OR FROM
LIVINGBOOKPRESS.COM

Handbook of Nature-Study:

Mammals and Flowerless Plants

ANNA BOTSFORD COMSTOCK, B.S., L.H.D

LATE PROFESSOR OF NATURE-STUDY IN CORNELL UNIVERSITY

LIVING BOOK
PRESS

This edition published 2020
by Living Book Press

ISBN: 978-1-922348-64-7 (hardcover)
        978-1-922348-65-4 (softcover)

A catalogue record for this
book is available from the
National Library of Australia

CONTENTS

MAMMALS

FLOWERLESS PLANTS

MAMMALS

Human beings are are mammals

MAMMALS

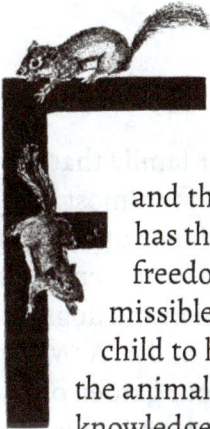

FOR some inexplicable reason, the word animal, in common parlance, is restricted to the mammals. As a matter of fact, the bird, the fish, the insect, and the snake have as much right to be called animals as has the squirrel or the deer. And while I believe that much freedom in the matter of scientific nomenclature is permissible in nature-study, I also believe that it is well for the child to have a clearly defined idea of the classes into which the animal kingdom is divided; and I would have him gain this knowledge by noting how one animal differs from another rather than by studying the classification of animals in books. He sees that the fish differs in many ways from the bird and that the toad differs from the snake; and it will be easy for him to grasp the fact that the mammals differ from all other animals in that the young are nourished by milk produced for this purpose in the breasts of the mother; when he understands this, he can comprehend how such diverse forms as the whale, the cow, the bat, and human beings are akin.

The Cotton-Tail Rabbit

TEACHER'S STORY

"The Bunnies are a feeble folk whose weakness is their strength.
To shun a gun a Bun will run to almost any length."
—Oliver Herford

IT IS well for Molly Cotton-tail and her family that they have learned to shun more than guns for almost every predatory animal and bird makes a dinner of them on every possible occasion. But despite these enemies, moreover, with the addition of guns, men and dogs, the cotton-tail lives and flourishes in our midst. A "Molly" raised two families last year in a briar-patch back of our garden on the Cornell Campus, where dogs of many breeds abound; and after each fresh fall of snow this winter we have been able to trace our bunny neighbors in their night wanderings around the house, beneath the spruces and in the orchard. The track consists of two long splashes, paired, and between and a little behind them, two smaller ones; the rabbit uses its front feet as a boy uses a vaulting pole and lands both hind feet on each side and ahead of them; owing to the fact that the bottoms of the feet are hairy the print is not clear-cut. When the rabbit is not in a hurry it has a peculiar lope, but when frightened it makes long jumps. The cotton-tails are night wanderers and usually remain hidden during the day. In summer, they feed on clover or grass or other juicy herbs and show a fondness for sweet apples and fresh cabbage; in our garden last summer Molly was very considerate. She carefully pulled all the grass out of the garden-cress bed, leaving the salad for our enjoyment.

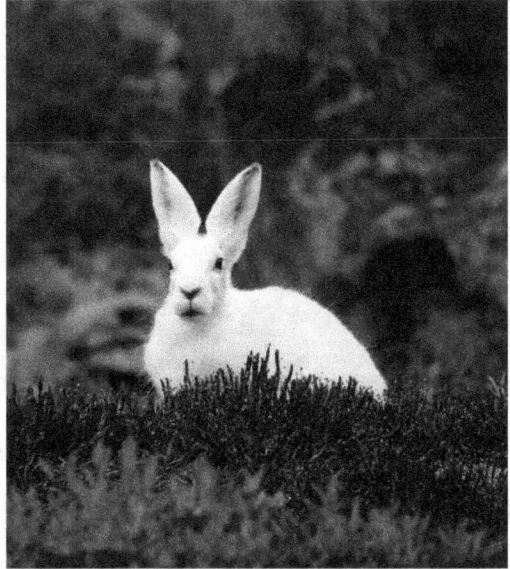

The rabbits' ears are ever alert for any sign of danger

In winter, the long, gnawing teeth of the cotton-tail are sometimes used to the damage of fruit trees and nursery stock since the rabbits are obliged to feed upon bark in order to keep alive.

The long, strong hind legs and the long ears tell the whole bunny story. Ears to hear the approach of the enemy, and legs to propel the listener by long jumps to a safe retreat. The attitude of the ears is a good indication of the bunny's state of mind; if they are set back to back and directed backward, they indicate placidity, but a placidity that is always on guard; if lifted straight up they signify attention and anxiety; if one is bent forward and the other backward the meaning is: "Now just where did that sound come from?" When running or when resting in the form, the ears are laid back along the neck. When the cotton-tail stands up on its haunches with both ears erect, it looks very tall indeed.

Not only are the ears always alert, but also the nose; the nostrils are partially covered and in order to be always sure of getting every scent they wabble constantly, the split upper lip aiding in this performance; when the rabbit is trying to get a scent it moves its head up and down in a sagacious, apprehensive manner.

The rabbit has an upper and lower pair of incisors like other ro-

A dutch rabbit

dents, but on the upper jaw there is a short incisor on each side of the large teeth; these are of no use now but are inherited from some ancestor which found them useful. There are at the back of each side of the upper jaw six grinding teeth, and five on each side of the lower jaw. The split upper lip allows the free use of the upper incisors. The incisors are not only used for taking the bark from trees, but also for cutting grass and other food. The rabbit has a funny way of taking a stem of grass or clover at the end and with much wabbling of lips, finally taking it in, meanwhile chewing it with a sidewise motion of the jaws. The rabbits' whiskers are valuable as feelers, and are always kept on the *qui vive* for impressions; when two cotton-tails meet each other amicably, they rub whiskers together. The eyes are large and dark and placed on the bulge at the side of the head, so as to command the view both ways. Probably a cotton-tail winks, but I never caught one in the act.

The strong hind legs of the rabbit enable it to make prodigious jumps, of eight feet or more; this is a valuable asset to an animal that escapes its enemies by running. The front feet are short and cannot be turned inward like those of the squirrel, to hold food. There are five toes on the front feet, and four on the hind feet; the hair on the bottom of the feet is a protection, much needed by an animal which sits for long periods upon the snow. When sleeping, the front paws are folded under and the rabbit rests on the entire hind foot, with the knee bent, ready for a spring at the slightest alarm; when awake, it rests on the hind feet and front toes; and when it wishes to see if the coast is clear, it rises on its hind feet, with front paws drooping.

Wild rabbits on a lawn

The cotton-tail has a color well calculated to protect it from observation; it is brownish-gray on the back and a little lighter along the sides, grayish under the chin and whitish below; the ears are edged with black, and the tail when raised shows a large, white fluff at the rear. The general color of the rabbit fits in with natural surroundings; since the cotton-tail often escapes its enemies by "freezing," this color makes the scheme work well. I once saw a marsh hare, on a stone in a brook, freezing most successfully. I could hardly believe that a living thing could seem so much like a stone; only its bright eyes revealed it to us.

The rabbit cleans itself in amusing ways. It shakes its feet, one at a time, with great vigor and rapidity to get off the dirt and then licks them clean. It washes its face with both front paws at once. It scratches its ear with the hind foot, and pushes it forward so that it can be licked; it takes hold of its fur with its front feet to pull it around within reach of the tongue.

The cotton-tail does not dig a burrow, but sometimes occupies the deserted burrow of a woodchuck or skunk. Its nest is called a "form," which simply means a place beneath a cover of grass or briars, where the grass is beaten down or eaten out for a space large enough for the animal to sit. The mother makes a soft bed for the young, using grass and her own hair for the purpose; and she constructs a coarse felted coverlet, under which she tucks her babies with care, every time she leaves them. Young rabbits are blind at first, but when about three weeks old, are sufficiently grown to run quite rapidly. Although there may be five or six in a litter, yet there are so many enemies that only a few escape.

Washing up

Fox, mink, weasel, hawk, owl and snake all relish the young cottontail if they can get it. Nothing but its runways through the briars can save it. These roads wind in and out and across, twisting and turning perplexingly; they are made by cutting off the grass stems, and are just wide enough for the rabbit's body. However, a rabbit has weapons and can fight if necessary; it leaps over its enemy, kicking it on the back fiercely with its great hind feet. Mr. Seton tells of this way of conquering the black snake, and Mr. Sharp saw a cat completely vanquished by the same method. The rabbit can also bite, and when two males are fighting, they bite each other savagely. Mr. E. W. Cleeves told me of a Belgian doe which showed her enmity to cats in a peculiar way. She would run after any cats that came in sight, butting them like a billy-goat. The cats soon learned her tricks, and would climb a tree as soon as they caught sight of her. The rabbit's sound of defiance, is thumping the ground with the strong hind foot. Some have declared that the front feet are used also for stamping; although I have heard this indignant thumping more than once, I could not see the process. The cotton-tail is a hare, while the common domestic rabbit is a true rabbit. The two differ chiefly in the habits of nesting; the hares rest and nest in forms, while the rabbit makes burrows, digging rapidly with the front feet.

Not the least of tributes to the rabbit's sagacity, are the negro folk-stories told by Uncle Remus, wherein Br'er Rabbit, although often in trouble, is really the most clever of all the animals. I have often thought when I have seen the tactics which rabbits have adopted to escape dogs, that we in the North have under-rated the cleverness of this timid animal. In one instance at least that came under our observation, a cotton-tail led a dog to the verge of a precipice, then doubled

Rabbit Tracks

Rabbits must be alert for danger

back to safety, while the dog went over, landing on the rocks nearly three hundred feet below.

LESSON

Leading thought— The cotton-tail thrives amid civilization; its color protects it from sight; its long ears give it warning of the approach of danger; and its long legs enable it to run by swift, long leaps. It feeds upon grasses, clover, vegetables and other herbs.

Method— This study may be begun in the winter, when the rabbit tracks can be observed and the haunts of the cotton-tail discovered. If caught in a box trap, the cotton-tail will become tame if properly fed and cared for, and may thus be studied at close range. The cage I have used for rabbits as thus caught, is made of wire screen, nailed to a frame, making a wire-covered box, two feet high and two or three feet square, with a door at one side and no bottom. It should be placed upon oil-cloth or linoleum, and thus may be moved to another carpet when the floor needs cleaning. If it is impossible to study the cotton-tail, the domestic rabbit may be used instead.

Observations—

1. What sort of tracks does the cotton-tail make in the snow? Describe and sketch them. Where do you find these tracks? How do you know which way the rabbit was going? Follow the track and see if you can find where the rabbit went. When were these tracks made, by night or by day? What does the rabbit do during the day? What does it find to eat during the winter? How are its feet protected so that they do not freeze in the snow?

2. What are the two most noticeable peculiarities of the rabbit? Of what use are such large ears? How are the ears held when the rabbit is resting? When startled? When not quite certain about the direction of the noise? Explain the reasons for these attitudes. When the rabbit wishes to make an observation to see if there is danger coming, what does it do? How does it hold its ears then? How are the ears held when the animal is running?

3. Do you think the rabbit has a keen sense of smell? Describe the movements of the nostrils and explain the reason. How does it move its head to be sure of getting the scent?

4. What peculiarity is there in the upper lip? How would this be an aid to the rabbit when gnawing? Describe the teeth; how do these differ from those of the mouse or squirrel? Of what advantage are the gnawing teeth to the rabbit? How does it eat a stem of grass? Note the rabbit's whiskers. What do you think they are used for?

5. Describe the eyes. How are they placed so that the rabbit can see forward and backward? Do you think that it sleeps with its eyes open? Does it wink?

6. Why is it advantageous to the rabbit to have such long, strong, hind legs? Compare them in size with the front legs. Compare the front and hind feet. How many toes on each? How are the bottoms of the feet protected? Are the front feet ever used for holding food like the squirrel's? In what position are the legs when the rabbit is resting? When it is standing? When lifted up for observation?

7. How does the cotton-tail escape being seen? Describe its coat. Of what use is the white fluff beneath the tail? Have you ever seen a wild rabbit "freeze"? What is meant by freezing and what is the use of it?

8. In making its toilet how does the rabbit clean its face, ears, feet, and fur?

9. What do the cotton-tails feed upon during the summer? During the winter? Do they ever do much damage?

10. Describe the cotton-tail's nest. What is it called? Does it ever burrow in the ground? Does it ever use a second-hand burrow? Describe the nest made for the young by the mother. Of what is the bed composed? Of what is the coverlet made? What is the special use of the coverlet? How do the young cotton-tails look? How old are they before they are able to take care of themselves?

11. What are the cotton-tail's enemies? How does it escape them? Have you ever seen the rabbit roads in a briar patch? Do you think that a dog or fox could follow them? Do rabbits ever fight their enemies? If so, how? How do they show anger? Do they stamp with the front or the hind foot?

12. Tell how the cotton-tail differs in looks and habits from the common tame rabbit. How do the latter dig their burrows? How many breeds of tame rabbits do you know?

13. Write or tell stories on the following topics: "A Cotton-tail's Story of its Own Life Until it is a Year Old;" "The Jack-rabbit of the West;" "The Habits of the White Rabbit or Varying Hare;" "The Rabbit in Uncle Remus' Tales."

Supplementary Reading— "Raggylug" and "Little War Horse," Thompson-Seton; *Squirrels and Other Fur-Bearers*, Burroughs; *Watchers in the Woods*, Sharp; *American Animals*, Stone & Cram; *Familiar Life in Field and Forest*, Mathews; *Sharp Eyes*, Gibson; *Neighbors with Claws and Hoofs*, Johonnot; *True Tales of Birds and Beasts*, Jordan; *Uncle Remus Stories*, especially The Tar Baby, which emphasizes the fact that the rabbits' runways are in the protecting briar-patch.

The Muskrat

"*Having finished this first course of big-neck clams, they were joined by a third muskrat, and, together, they filed over the bank and down into the meadow. Shortly two of them returned with great mouthfuls of the mud-bleached ends of calamus-blades. Then followed the washing.*

They dropped their loads upon the plank, took up the stalks, pulled the blades apart, and soused them up and down in the water, rubbing them with their paws until they were as clean and white as the whitest celery one ever ate. What a dainty picture! Two little brown creatures, humped on the edge of a plank, washing calamus in moonlit water!"

—DALLAS LORE SHARP

TRACKING is a part of every boy's education who aspires to a knowledge of wood lore; and a boy with this accomplishment is sure to be looked upon with great admiration by other boys, less skilled in the interpretation of that writing made by small feet, on the soft snow or on the mud of stream margins. To such a boy, the track of the muskrat is well known, and very easily recognized.

The muskrat is essentially a water animal, and therefore its tracks are to be looked for along the edges of ponds, streams or in marshes. Whether the tracks are made by walking or jumping, depends upon the depth of the snow or mud; if it is deep, the animal jumps, but in shallow snow or mud, it simply runs along. The tracks show the front feet to be smaller than the hind ones. The muskrat track is, however, characterized by the tail imprint. When the creature jumps through the snow, the mark of the tail follows the paired imprints of the feet; when it walks, there is a continuous line made by this strong, naked tail. This distinguishes the track of the muskrat from that of the mink, as the bushy tail of the latter does not make so distinct a mark. Measuring the track, is simply a device for making the pupils note its size and shape more carefully. The tracks may be looked for during the thaws of March or February, when the muskrats come out of the water to seek food.

In appearance the muskrat is peculiar. The body is usually about a foot in length and the tail about eight inches. The body is stout and thickset, the head is rounded and looks like that of a giant meadow mouse; the eyes are black and shining; the ears are short and close to the head; the teeth, like those of other rodents, consist of a pair of front teeth on each jaw, then a long, bare space and four grinders on each side. There are long sensitive hairs about the nose and mouth, like the whiskers of mice.

The muskrat's hind legs are much larger and stronger than the front ones; and too, the hind feet are much longer than the front feet and have a web between the toes; there are also stiff hairs which fill the space between the toes, outside the web, thus making this large hind foot an excellent swimming organ. The front toes are not webbed and are used for digging. The claws are long, stout and sharp. The tail is long, stout and flattened at the sides; it has little or no fur upon it but is covered with scales; it is used as a scull and also as a rudder when the muskrat is swimming.

The muskrat's outer coat consists of long, rather coarse hairs; its

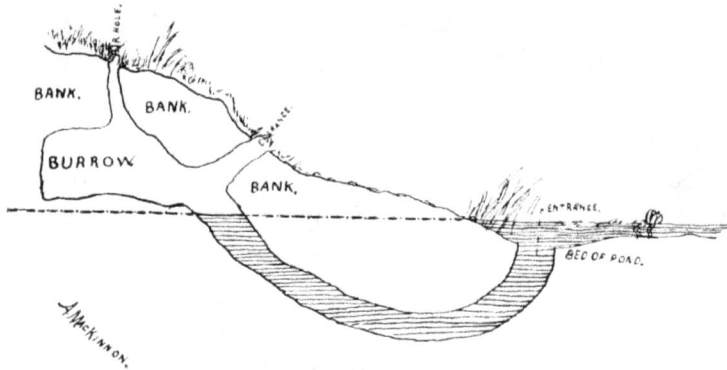

A Muskrat's Summer Home
Drawn by A. MacKinnon, a boy of 13 years.

under coat is of fur, very thick and fine, and although short, it forms a waterproof protection for the body of the animal. In color, the fur is dark brown above with a darker streak along the middle of the back; beneath, the body is grayish changing to whitish on the throat and lips, with a brown spot on the chin. In preparing the pelts for commercial use, the long hairs are plucked out leaving the soft, fine under coat, which is dyed and sold under the name of "electric seal."

The muskrat is far better fitted by form, for life in the water than upon the land. Since it is heavy-bodied and short-legged, it cannot run rapidly but its strong, webbed hind feet are most efficient oars, and it swims rapidly and easily; for rudder and propeller the strong, flattened tail serves admirably, while the fine fur next the body is so perfectly waterproof that, however much the muskrat swims or dives, it is never wet. It is a skillful diver and can stay under water for several minutes; when swimming, its nose and sometimes the head and the tip of the tail appear on the surface of the water.

The food of muskrats is largely roots, especially those of the sweet flag and the yellow lily. They also feed on other aquatic plants and are fond of the fresh-water shell-fish. Mr. Sharp tells us, in one of his delightful stories, how the muskrats wash their food by sousing it up and down in water many times before eating it. Often, a muskrat chooses some special place upon the shore which it uses for a dining-room, bringing there and eating pieces of lily root or fresh-water clams, and leaving the debris to show where it habitually dines. It does most of

A muskrat lodge

its hunting for food at night, although sometimes it may be seen thus employed during the day.

The winter lodge of the muskrat is a most interesting structure. A foundation of tussocks of rushes, in a stream or shallow pond, is built upon with reeds plastered with mud, making a rather regular dome which may be nearly two or three feet high; or, if many-chambered, it may be a grand affair of four or five feet elevation; but it always looks so much like a natural hummock that the eye of the uninitiated never regards it as a habitation. Always beneath this dome and above the water line, is a snug, covered chamber carpeted with a soft bed of leaves and moss, which has a passage leading down into the water below, and also has an air-hole for ventilation. In these cabins, closely cuddled together, three or four in a chamber, the muskrats pass the winter. After the pond is frozen they are safe from their enemies and are always able to go down into the water and feed upon the roots of water plants. These cabins are sometimes built in the low, drooping branches of willows or on other objects.

Whether the muskrat builds itself a winter lodge or not, depends upon the nature of the shore which it inhabits; if it is a place particularly fitted for burrows, then a burrow will be used as a winter retreat; but if the banks are shallow, the muskrats unite in building cabins. The main entrance to the muskrat burrow is always below the surface of the water, the burrow slanting upward and leading to a nest well

A beaver. The habits of beavers somewhat resemble those of muskrats. Beavers may weigh from 40 to 60 pounds and reach a length of 40 inches. In North America they range from Hudson Bay and Alaska south into Mexico in the West and the southern Alleghenies in the East

lined, which is above the reach of high water; there is always an air hole above, for ventilating this nest, and there is also often a passage, with a hidden entrance, leading out to dry land.

The flesh of the muskrat is delicious, and therefore the animal has many enemies; foxes, weasels, dogs, minks and also hawks and owls prey upon it. It escapes the sight of its enemies as does the mouse, by having the color of its fur not noticeable; when discovered, it escapes its enemies by swimming, although when cornered, it is courageous and fights fiercely, using its strong incisors as weapons. In winter, it dwells in safety when the friendly ice protects it from all its enemies except the mink; but it is exposed to great danger when the streams break up in spring, for it is then often driven from its cabin by floods, and preyed upon while thus helplessly exposed. The muskrat gives warning of danger to its fellows by splashing the water with its strong tail.

It is called muskrat because of the odor, somewhat resembling musk, which it exhales from two glands on the lower side of the body between the hind legs; these glands may be seen when the skin is removed, which is the too common plight of this poor creature, since it is hunted mercilessly for its pelt.

The little muskrats are born in April and there are usually from six to eight in a litter. Another litter may be produced in June or July and a third in August

A beaver lodge

or September. It is only thus, by rearing large families often, that the muskrats are able to hold their own against the hunters and trappers and their natural enemies.

References— *Wild Animals,* Stone & Cram; *A Watcher in the Woods,* Sharp; *Wild Life,* Ingersoll; Farmers' Bulletin No. 396, U. S. Dept. of Agriculture.

LESSON

Leading thought— The muskrat, while a true rodent, is fitted for life in the water more than for life upon the land. Its hind feet are webbed for use as oars and its tail is used as a rudder. It builds lodges of mud, cat-tails and rushes in which it spends the winter.

Method— It might be well to begin this work by asking for observations on the tracks of the muskrat which may be found about the edges of almost any creek, pond or marsh. If there are muskrat lodges in the region they should be visited and described. For studying the muskrat's form a live muskrat in captivity is almost necessary. If one is trapped with a "figure four" it will not be injured and it may be made more or less tame by feeding it with sweet apples, carrots and parsnips. The pupils can thus study it at leisure although they should not be allowed to handle the creature as it inflicts very severe wounds and is never willing to be handled. If a live muskrat cannot be obtained perhaps some hunter in the neighborhood will supply a dead one for this observation lesson.

Trees felled by beavers. Unlike muskrats, beavers fell trees. They have cut these birches either to use the bark for food or the trunks for reinforcement of a dam.

While studying the muskrat the children should read all the stories of beavers which are available as the two animals are very much alike in their habits.

Observations—

1. In what locality have you discovered the tracks of the muskrat? Describe its general appearance. Measure the muskrat's track as follows: (a) Width and length of the print of one foot; (b) the width between the prints of the two hind feet; (c) the length between the prints made by the hind feet in several successive steps or jumps.

2. Was the muskrat's track made when the animal was jumping or walking? Can you see in it a difference in the size of the front and hind feet? Judging from the track, where do you think the muskrat came from? What do you think it was hunting for?

3. What mark does the tail make in the snow or mud? Judging by its imprint, should you think the muskrat's tail was long or short, bare or brushy, slender or strong?

4. How long is the largest muskrat you ever saw? How much of the whole length is tail? Is the general shape of the body short and heavy or long and slender?

5. Describe the muskrat's eyes, ears and teeth. For what are the teeth especially fitted? Has the muskrat whiskers like mice and rats?

6. Compare the front and hind legs as to size and shape. Is there a web between the toes of the hind feet? What does this indicate? Do you think that the muskrat is a good swimmer?

7. Describe the muskrat fur. Compare the outer and under coat. What is its color above and below? What is the name of muskrat fur in the shops?

8. Describe the tail. What is its covering? How is it flattened? What do you think this strong, flattened tail is used for?

9. Do you think the muskrat is better fitted to live in the water than on land? How is it fitted to live in the water in the following particulars: Feet? Tail? Fur?

10. How much of the muskrat can you see when it is swimming? How long can it stay under water when diving?

11. What is the food of the muskrat? Where does it find it? How does it prepare the food for eating? Does it seek its food during the night or day? Have you ever observed the muskrat's dining room? If so, describe it.

12. Describe the structure of the muskrat's winter lodge, or cabin, in the following particulars: Its size. Where built? Of what material? How many rooms in it? Are these rooms above or below the water level? Of what is the bed made? How is the nest ventilated? How is it arranged so that the entrance is not closed by the ice? Is such a home built by one or more muskrats? How many live within it? Do the muskrats always build these winter cabins? What is the character of the shores where they are built?

13. Describe the muskrat's burrow in the bank in the following particulars: Is the entrance above or below water? Where and how is the nest made? Is it ventilated? Does it have a back door leading out upon the land?

14. What are the muskrat's enemies? How does it escape them? How does it fight? Is it a courageous animal? How does the muskrat give warning to its fellows when it perceives danger? At what time of year is it comparatively safe? At what time is it exposed to greatest danger?

Notice the strong teeth of the beaver

15. Why is this animal called muskrat? Compare the habits of muskrats with those of beaver and write an English theme upon the similarity of the two.

16. At what time of year do you find the young muskrats? How many in a litter?

17. Read Farmers' Bulletin No. 396 of the U. S. Dept. of Agriculture and write an English theme on the destructive habits of muskrats and the economic uses of these animals.

Supplementary reading— Familiar Wild Animals, Lottridge; Little Beasts of Field and Wood, Cram; Squirrels and Other Fur-Bearers, Burroughs; "The Builders" in Ways of Wood Folk, Long.

The House Mouse

TEACHER'S STORY

Somewhere in the darkness a clock strikes two;
And there is no sound in the sad old house,
But the long veranda dripping with dew,
And in the wainscot—a mouse.

—*BRET HARTE*

WERE mouse-gray a less inconspicuous color, there would be fewer mice; when a mouse is running along the floor, it is hardly discernible, it looks so like a flitting shadow; if it were black or white or any other color, it would be more often seen and destroyed. Undoubtedly, it is owing to the fact that its soft fur has this shadowy color, that this species has been able to spread over the world.

At first glance one wonders what possible use a mouse can make of a tail which is as long as its body, but a little careful observation will

Young pet mice, still blind by getting their first hair

reveal the secret. The tail is covered with transverse ridges and is bare save for sparse hairs, except toward the tip. Dr. Ida Reveley first called my attention to the fact that the house mouse uses its tail in climbing. I verified this interesting observation, and found that my mouse used the tail for aid when climbing a string. He would go up the string, hand over hand, like a sailor, then in trying to stretch to the edge of his jar, he invariably wound his tail about the string two or three times, and hanging to the string with the hind feet and tail, would reach far out with his head and front feet. Also, when clinging to the edge of the cover of the jar, he invariably used his tail as a brace against the side of the glass, so that it pressed hard for more than half its length. Undoubtedly the tail is of great service when climbing up the sides of walls.

The tail is also of some use, when the mouse jumps directly upwards. The hind legs are very much longer and stronger than the front legs. The hind feet are also much longer and larger than the front feet; and although the mouse, when it makes its remarkable jumps, depends upon its strong hind legs, I am sure that often the tail is used as a brace to guide and assist the leap. The feet are free from hairs but are downy; the hind foot has three front toes, a long toe behind on the outside and a short one on the inside. The claws are fairly long and very sharp so that they are able to cling to almost anything but glass. When exploring, a mouse stands on its hind feet, folding its little front paws under its chin while it reaches up ready to catch anything in sight; it can stretch up to an amazing height. It feeds upon almost anything which people like to eat and, when eating, holds its food in its front paws like a squirrel.

The thin, velvety ears are flaring cornucopias for taking in sound;

the large, rounded outer ear can be moved forward or back to test the direction of the noise. The eyes are like shining, black beads; and if a mouse can wink, it does it so rapidly as not to be discernible. The nose is long, inquisitive, and always sniffing for new impressions.

A white-footed or deer mouse may use an old bird's nest for its home

The whiskers are delicate and probably sensitive. The mouth is furnished with two long, curved gnawing teeth at the front of each jaw, then a bare space, and four grinding teeth on each side, above and below, like the teeth of woodchucks and other rodents. The gnawing teeth are very strong and enable the mouse to gnaw through board partitions and other obstacles.

The energy with which the mouse cleans itself is inspiring to behold. It nibbles its fur and licks it with fervor, reaching around so as to get at it from behind, and taking hold with its little hands to hold firm while it cleans. When washing its face and head, it uses both front feet, licking them clean and rubbing them both simultaneously from behind the ears down over the face. It takes its hind foot in both front feet and nibbles and licks it. It scratches the back of its head with its hind foot.

Young mice are small, downy, pink and blind when born. The mother makes for them a nice, soft nest of pieces of cloth, paper, grass, or whatever is at hand; the nest is round like a ball and at its center is nestled the family. Mice living in houses, have runways between the plaster and the outside, or between ceiling and floor. In winter they live on what food they can find, and upon flies or other insects hibernating in our houses. The house mice sometimes live under stacks of corn or grain in the fields, but usually confine themselves to houses or barns. They are thirsty little fellows and they like to make their nests within easy reach of water. Our house mice came from ancestors which lived in Asia originally; they have always been great travelers and they have

Tracks of a white-footed mouse
Notice tail-track

followed men wherever they have gone, over the world. They came to America on ships with the first explorers and the Pilgrim fathers. They now travel back and forth, crossing the ocean in ships of all sorts. They also travel across the continent on trains. Wherever our food is carried they go; and the mouse, which you see in your room one day, may be a thousand miles away within a week. They are clever creatures, and learn quickly to connect cause and effect. For two years, I was in an office in Washington, and as soon as the bell rang for noon, the mice would appear instantly, hunting waste-baskets for scraps of lunch. They had learned to connect the sound of the bell with food.

Of all our wild mice, the white-footed or deer mouse is the most interesting and attractive. It is found almost exclusively in woods and is quite different in appearance from other mice. Its ears are very large; its fur is fine and beautiful and a most delicate gray color. It is white beneath the head and under the sides of the body. The feet are pinkish, the front paws have short thumbs, while the hind feet are very much longer and have a long thumb looking very much like an elfin hand in a gray-white silk glove. On the bottom of the feet are callous spots which are pink and serve as foot pads. It makes its nest in hollow trees and stores nuts for winter use. We once found two quarts of shelled beech nuts in such a nest. It also likes the hips of the wild rose and many kinds of berries; it sometimes makes its summer home in a bird's nest, which it roofs over to suit itself. The young mice are carried, hanging to the mother's breasts. As an inhabitant of summer cottages, white-foot is cunning and mischievous; it pulls cotton out of quilts, takes covers off of jars, and as an explorer, is equal to the squirrel. I once tried to rear some young deer mice by feeding them warm milk with a pipette; although their eyes were not open, they invariably washed their faces after each meal, showing that neatness was bred in the bone. This mouse has a musical voice and often chirps as sweetly as a bird. Like the house mouse it is more active at night.

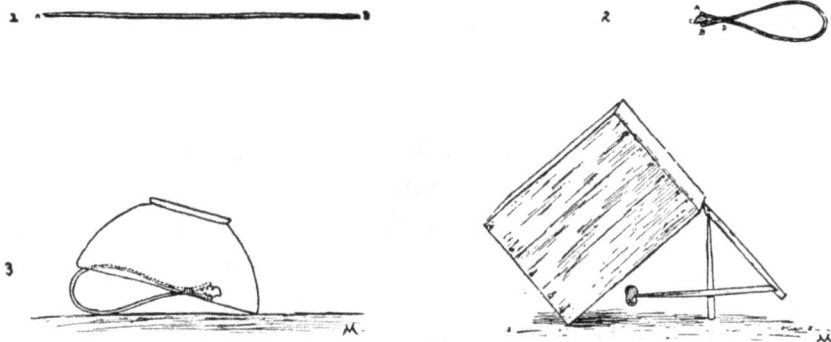

Mouse Traps
1. Bow Trap—A smooth splint or a peeled twig.
2. Bow Trap—Splint bowed and tied at D, the bait inserted at C.
3. Bow Trap—The inverted bowl balanced on splint bow.
4. Trap

The meadow mouse is the one that makes its run-ways under the snow, making strange corrugated patterns over the ground which attract our attention in spring. It has a heavy body, short legs, short ears and short tail. It is brownish or blackish in color. It sometimes digs burrows straight into the ground, but more often makes its nest beneath sticks and stones or stacks of corn. It is the nest of this field mouse which the bumblebee so often takes possession of, after it is deserted. The meadow mouse is a good fighter, sitting up like a woodchuck and facing its enemy bravely. It needs to be courageous, for it is preyed upon by almost every creature that feeds upon small animals; the hawks and owls especially are its enemies. It is well for the farmer that these mice have so many enemies, for they multiply rapidly and would otherwise soon overrun and destroy the grain fields. This mouse is an excellent swimmer.

A part of winter work, is to make the pupils familiar with the tracks of the meadow mice and how to distinguish them from other tracks.

Trapping Field Mice— Probably wild animals have endured more cruelty through the agency of traps than through any other form of human persecution. The savage steel traps often catch the animal by the leg, holding it until it gnaws off the imprisoned foot, and thus escapes maimed and handicapped for its future struggle for food; or if the trap gets a strong hold, the poor creature may suffer tortures during a long period, before the owner of the trap appears to put an end to its sufferings by death. If box traps are used, they are often neglected and the poor creature imprisoned, is left to languish and starve. The teacher cannot enforce too strongly upon the child the ethics of trapping. Impress upon him that the box traps are far less cruel; but that if set, they must be examined regularly and not neglected. The study of mice affords a good opportunity for giving the children a lesson in humane trapping. Let them set a figure 4 or a bowl trap, which they must examine every morning. The little prisoners may be brought to school and studied; meanwhile, they should be treated kindly and fed bountifully. After a mouse has been studied, it should be set free, even though it be one of the quite pestiferous field mice. The moral effect of killing an animal, after a child has become thoroughly interested in it and its life, is always bad.

References— *Claws and Hoofs*, Johonnot; *American Animals*, Stone & Cram; *Secrets of the Woods*, Long; *Wild Life*, Ingersoll; *Familiar Wild Animals*, Lottridge.

LESSON

Leading thought— The mouse is fitted by color, form, agility and habits to thrive upon the food which it steals from man, and to live in the midst of civilized people.

Method— A mouse cage can be easily made of wire window-screen tacked upon a wooden frame. I have even used aquarium jars with wire screen covers, and by placing one jar upon another, opening to opening, and then laying them horizontal, the mouse can be transferred to a fresh cage without trouble, and thus the mousey odor can be obviated, while the little creature is being studied. A little water in a wide-necked bottle can be lowered into this glass house by a string, and the food can be given in like manner. Stripped paper should be put into the jar for the comfort of the prisoner; a stiff string hanging down from the middle of the cage will afford the prisoner a chance to show his feats as an acrobat.

Observations—

1. Why is the color of the mouse of special benefit to it? Do you think it protects it from the sight of its enemies? Can you see a mouse eas-

ily as it runs across the room? What is the nature of the fur of a mouse?

2. How long is a mouse's tail as compared with its body? What is the covering of the tail? Of what use to the mouse is this long, ridged tail? Watch the mouse carefully and discover, if you can, the use of the tail in climbing.

3. Is the mouse a good jumper? Are the hind legs long and strong when compared with the front legs? How high do you think a mouse can jump? Do you think it uses its tail as an aid in jumping? How much of the legs are covered with hair? Compare the front and hind feet. What sort of claws have they? How does the mouse use its feet when climbing the string? How can it climb up the side of a wall?

4. Describe the eyes. Do you think the mouse can see very well? Does it wink? What is the shape of the ears? Do you think it can hear well? Can it move its ears forward or backward?

5. What is the shape of the snout? Of what advantage is this? Note the whiskers. What is their use? Describe the mouth. Do you know how the teeth are arranged? For what other use than to bite food does the mouse use its teeth? What other animals have their teeth arranged like those of the mouse? What food does the house mouse live upon? How does it get it?

6. How does the mouse act when it is reaching up to examine something? How does it hold its front feet? Describe how the mouse washes its face. Its back. Its feet.

7. Where does the house mouse build its nest? Of what material? How do the baby mice look? Can they see when they are first born?

8. House mice are great travelers. Can you tell how they manage to get from place to place? Write a story telling all you know of their habits.

9. How many kinds of mice do you know? Does the house mouse ever live in the field? What do you know of the habits of the white-footed mouse? Of the meadow mice? Of the jumping mice?

The Woodchuck

H E who knows the ways of the woodchuck can readily guess where it is likely to be found; it loves meadows and pastures where grass or clover lushly grows. It is also fond of garden truck and has a special delectation for melons. The burrow is likely to be situated near a fence or stone heap, which gives easy access to the chosen food. The woodchuck makes its burrow by digging the earth loose with its front feet, and pushing it backward and out of the entrance with the hind feet. This method leaves the soil in a heap near the entrance, from which paths radiate into the grass in all directions. If one undertakes to dig out a woodchuck, one needs to be not only a husky individual, but something of an engineer; the direction of the burrow extends downward for a little way, and then rises at an easy angle, so that the inmate may be in no danger of flood. The nest is merely an enlargement of the burrow, lined with soft grass, which the woodchucks bring in in their mouths. During the early part of the season, the father and mother and the litter of young may inhabit the same

28

burrow, although there are likely to be at least two separate nests. There is usually more than one back door to the woodchuck's dwelling, through which it may escape, if pressed too closely by enemies; these back doors differ from the entrance, in that they are usually hidden and have no earth heaped near them.

The woodchuck usually feeds in the morning and again in the evening, and is likely to spend the middle of the day resting. It often goes some distance from

The woodchuck is at home in grassy meadows

its burrow to feed, and at short intervals, lifts itself upon its hind feet to see if the coast is clear; if assailed, it will seek to escape by running to its burrow; and when running, it has a peculiar gait well described as "pouring itself along." If it reaches its burrow, it at once begins to dig deeply and throw the earth out behind it, thus making a wall to keep out the enemy. When cornered, the woodchuck is a courageous and fierce fighter; its sharp incisors prove a powerful weapon and it will often whip a dog much larger than itself. Every boy knows how to find whether the woodchuck is in its den or not, by rolling a stone into the burrow, and listening; if the animal is at home, the sound of its digging apprises the listener of the fact. In earlier times, the ground-hogs were much preyed upon by wolves, wildcats and foxes; now, only the fox remains and he is fast disappearing, so that at present, the farmer and his dog are about the only enemies this burrower has to contend with. It is an animal of resources and will climb a tree if attacked by a dog; it will also climb trees for fruit, like peaches. During the late summer, it is the ground-hog's business to feed very constantly and become very fat. About the first of October, it retires to its

Clover is a preferred food for groundhogs

den and sleeps until the end of March or April. During this dormant state, the beating of its heart is so faint as to be scarcely perceptible, and very little nourishment is required to keep it alive; this nourishment is supplied by the fat stored in its body, which it uses up by March, and comes out of its burrow in the spring, looking gaunt and lean. The old saying that the ground-hog comes out on Candlemas Day, and if it sees its shadow, goes back to sleep for six weeks more, may savor of meteorological truth, but it is certainly not true of the ground-hog.

The full-grown woodchuck ordinarily measures about two feet in length. Its color is grizzly or brownish, sometimes blackish in places; the under parts are reddish and the feet black. The fur is rather coarse, thick and brown, with longer hairs which are grayish. The skin is very thick and tough and seems to fit loosely, a condition which gives the peculiar "pouring along" appearance when it is running. The hind legs and feet are longer than those in front. Both pairs of feet are fitted for digging, the front ones being used for loosening the earth and the hind pair for kicking it out of the burrow.

The woodchuck's ears are roundish and not prominent, and by muscular contraction they are closed when the animal is digging, so that no soil can enter; the sense of hearing is acute. The teeth consist of two large incisors at the front of each jaw, a bare space and four grinders on each side, above and below; the incisors are used for biting food and also for fighting. The eyes are full and bright. The tail is short and brushy, and it with the hind legs, form a tripod which supports the animal, as it sits with its forefeet lifted.

When feeding, the woodchuck often makes a contented grunting noise; when attacked and fighting, it growls; and when feeling happy and conversational, it sits up and whistles. I had a woodchuck acquaintance once which always gave a

Groundhog with mouthful of burrow material

high, shrill, almost birdlike whistle when I came in view, a very jolly greeting. There are plenty of statements in books that woodchucks are fond of music, and Mr. Ingersoll states that at Wellesley College a woodchuck on the chapel lawn was wont to join the morning song exercises with a "clear soprano." The young woodchucks are born about the first of May and the litter usually numbers four or five. In June the "chucklings" may be seen following the mother in the field with much babyish grunting. If captured at this period, they make very interesting pets. By August or September the young woodchucks leave the home burrow and start burrows of their own.

References— *Wild Animals*, Stone & Cram; *Wild Neighbors*, Ingersoll; *Squirrels and Other Fur-Bearers*, Burroughs; *Familiar Wild Animals*, Lottridge.

LESSON

Leading thought— The woodchuck has thriven with civilization, notwithstanding the farmer's dog, gun, traps and poison. It makes its nest in a burrow in the earth and lives upon vegetation; it hibernates in winter.

Method— Within convenient distance for observation by the pupils of every country schoolhouse and of most village schoolhouses, may be found a woodchuck and its dwelling. The pupils should be given the outline for observations which should be made individually through watching the woodchuck for weeks or months.

Groundhogs playing

Observations—

1. Where is the woodchuck found? On what does it live? At what time of day does it feed? How does it act when startled?

2. Is the woodchuck a good fighter? With what weapons does it fight? What are its enemies? How does it escape its enemies when in or out of its burrow? How does it look when running?

3. What noises does the woodchuck make and what do they mean? Play a "mouth-organ" near the woodchuck's burrow and note if it likes music.

4. How does the woodchuck make its burrow? Where is it likely to be situated? Where is the earth placed which is taken from the burrow? How does the woodchuck bring it out? How is the burrow made so that the woodchuck is not drowned in case of heavy rains? In what direction do the underground galleries go? Where is the nest placed in relation to the galleries? Of what is the nest made? How is the bedding carried in? Of what special use is the nest?

5. Do you find paths leading to the entrances of the burrow? If so, describe them. How can you tell whether a woodchuck is at home or

not if you do not see it enter? Where is the woodchuck likely to station itself when it sits up to look for intruders?

6. How many woodchucks inhabit the same burrow? Are there likely to be one or more back doors to the burrow? What for? How do the back doors differ from the front doors?

7. How long is the longest woodchuck that you have ever seen? What is the woodchuck's color? Is its fur long or short? Coarse or fine? Thick or sparse? Is the skin thick or thin? Does it seem loose or close fitting?

8. Compare the front and hind feet and describe difference in size and shape. Are either or both slightly webbed? Explain how both front and hind feet and legs are adapted by their shape to help the wood-chuck. Is the tail long or short? How does it assist the animal in sitting up?

9. What is the shape of the woodchuck's ear? Can it hear well? Why are the ears not filled with soil when the animal is burrowing? Of what use are the long incisors? Describe the eyes.

10. How does the woodchuck prepare for winter? Where and how does it pass the winter? Did you ever know a woodchuck to come out on Candlemas Day to look for its shadow?

11. When does the woodchuck appear in the spring? Compare its general appearance in the fall and in the spring and explain the reason for the difference.

12. When are the young woodchucks born? What do you know of the way the mother woodchuck cares for her young?

As I turned round the corner of Hubbard's Grove, saw a woodchuck, the first of the season, in the middle of the field six or seven rods from the fence which bounds the wood, and twenty rods distant. I ran along the fence and cut him off, or rather overtook him, though he started at the same time. When I was only a rod and a half off, he stopped, and I did the same; then he ran again, and I ran up within three feet of him, when he stopped again, the fence being between us. I squatted down and surveyed him at my leisure. His eyes were dull black and rather inobvious, with a faint chestnut iris, with but little expression and that more of resignation than of anger. The general aspect was a coarse grayish brown, a sort of grisel. A lighter brown next the skin, then black or very

Groundhogs can climb trees to escape predators

dark brown and tipped with whitish rather loosely. The head between a squirrel and a bear, flat on the top and dark brown, and darker still or black on the tip of the nose. The whiskers black, two inches long. The ears very small and round-ish, set far back and nearly buried in the fur. Black feet, with long and slender claws for digging. It appeared to tremble, or perchance shivered with cold. When I moved, it gritted its teeth quite loud, sometimes striking the under jaw against the other chatteringly, sometimes grinding one jaw on the other, yet as if more from instinct than anger. Whichever way I turned, that way it headed. I took a twig a foot long and touched its snout, at which it started forward and bit the stick, lessening the distance between us to two feet, and still it held all the ground it gained. I played with it tenderly awhile with the stick, trying to open its gritting jaws. Ever its long incisors, two above and two below, were presented. But I thought it would go to sleep if I stayed long enough. It did not sit upright as sometimes, but standing on its fore feet with its head down, i.e., half sitting, half standing. We sat looking at one another about half an hour, till we began to feel mesmeric influences. When I was tired, I moved away, wishing to see him run, but I could not start him. He would not stir as long as I was looking at him or could see him. I walked around him; he turned as fast and fronted me still. I sat down by his side within a foot. I talked to him quasi forest lingo, baby-talk, at any rate in a conciliatory tone, and thought that I had some influence on him. He gritted his teeth less. I chewed checkerberry leaves and presented them to his nose at last without a grit; though I saw that by so much gritting of the teeth he had worn them rapidly and they were covered with a fine white powder, which, if you measured it thus, would have made his anger terrible. He did not mind any noise I might make. With a little stick I lifted one of his paws to examine it, and held it up at pleasure. I turned him over to see what color he was beneath (darker or most pusely brown), though he turned himself back again sooner than I could have wished. His tail was also brown, though not very dark, rat-tail like, with loose hairs standing out on all sides like a caterpillar brush. He had a rather mild look. I spoke kindly to him. I reached checkerberry leaves to his mouth. I stretched my hands over him, though he turned up his head and still gritted a little. I laid my hand on him, but immediately took it off again, instinct not being wholly overcome. If I had had a few fresh bean leaves, thus in advance of the season, I am sure I should have tamed him completely. It was a frizzly tail. His is a humble, terrestrial color like the partridge's, well concealed where dead wiry grass rises above darker brown or chestnut dead leaves—a modest color. If I had had some food, I should have ended with stroking him at my leisure. Could easily have wrapped him in my handkerchief. He was not fat nor particularly lean. I finally had to leave him without seeing him move from the place. A large, clumsy, burrowing squirrel. Arctomys, bear-mouse. I respect him as one of the natives. He lies there, by his color and habits so naturalized amid the dry leaves, the withered grass, and the bushes. A sound nap, too, he has enjoyed in his native fields, the past winter. I think I might learn some wisdom of him. His ancestors have lived here longer than mine. He is more thoroughly acclimated and naturalized than I. Bean leaves the red man raised for him, but he can do without them.

—THOREAU'S JOURNAL

The Red Squirrel or Chickaree

TEACHER'S STORY

Just a tawny glimmer, a dash of red and gray,
Was it a flitting shadow, or a sunbeam gone astray!
It glances up a tree trunk, and a pair of bright eyes glow
Where a little spy in ambush is measuring his foe.
I hear a mocking chuckle, then wrathful, he grows bold
And stays his pressing business to scold and scold and scold.

WE ought to yield admiring tribute to those animals which have been able to flourish in our midst despite man and his gun, this weapon being the most cowardly and unfair invention of the human mind. The only time that man has been a fair fighter, in combating his four-footed brethren, was when he fought them with a weapon which he wielded

36

in his hand. There is nothing in animal comprehension which can take into account a projectile, and much less a shot from a gun; but though it does not understand, it experiences a deathly fear at the noise. It is pathetic to note the hush in a forest that follows the sound of a gun; every song, every voice, every movement is stilled and every little heart filled with nameless terror. How any man or boy can feel manly when, with this scientific instrument of death in his hands, he takes the life of a little squirrel, bird or rabbit, is beyond my comprehension. In pioneer days when it was a fight for existence,

CONNORMAH (CC BY-SA 3.0)
Red squirrel eating a nut

man against the wilderness, the matter was quite different; but now it seems to me that anyone who hunts what few wild creatures we have left, and which are in nowise injurious, is, whatever he may think of himself, no believer in fair play.

Within my own memory, the beautiful black squirrel was as common in our woods as was his red cousin; the shot-gun has exterminated this splendid species. Well may we rejoice that the red squirrel has, through its lesser size and greater cunning, escaped a like fate; and that pugnacious and companionable and shy, it lives in our midst and climbs our very roofs to sit there and scold us for coming within its range of vision. It has succeeded not only in living despite of man, but because of man, for it rifles our grain bins and corn cribs and waxes opulent by levying tribute upon our stores.

Thoreau describes most graphically the movements of this squir-

Midden (burrow) constructed by red squirrels in a spruce/birch forest.

rel. He says: "All day long the red squirrels came and went. One would approach at first warily, warily, through the shrub-oaks, running over the snow crust by fits and starts and like a leaf blown by the wind, now a few paces this way, with wonderful speed and waste of energy, making inconceivable haste with his "trotters," as if it were for a wager, and now as many paces that way, but never getting on more than half a rod at a time; and then suddenly pausing with a ludicrous expression and a gratuitous somersault, as if all the eyes of the universe were fixed on him… and then suddenly, before you could say Jack Robinson he would be in the top of a young pitch pine, winding up his clock, and chiding all imaginary spectators, soliloquizing and talking to all the universe at the same time."

It is surely one of the most comical of sights to see a squirrel stop running and take observations; he lifts himself on his haunches, and with body bent forward, presses his little paws against his breast as if to say, "Be still, oh my beating heart!" which is all pure affectation because he knows he can scurry away in perfect safety. He is likely to take refuge on the far side of a tree, peeping out from this side and that, and whisking back like a flash as he catches our eye; we might never know he was there except as Riley puts it, "he lets his own tail tell on him." When climbing up or down a tree, he goes head first and spreads his legs apart to clasp as much of the trunk as possible; meanwhile his sharp little claws cling securely to the bark. He can climb out on the smallest twigs quite as well, when he needs to do so, in passing from tree to tree or when gathering acorns.

A squirrel always establishes certain roads to and from his abiding place and almost invariably follows them. Such a path may be entirely in the treetops, with air bridges from a certain branch of one tree to a certain branch of another, or it may be partially on the ground between

A red squirrel swimming

trees. I have made notes of these paths in the vicinity of my own home, and have noted that if a squirrel leaves them for exploring, he goes warily; while, when following them, he is quite reckless in his haste. When making a jump from tree to tree, he flattens himself as widely as possible and his tail is held somewhat curved, but on a level with the body, as if its wide brush helped to buoy him up and perhaps to steer him also.

During the winter the chickaree is quite dingy in color and is an inconspicuous object, especially when he "humps himself up" so that he resembles a knot on a limb; but with the coming of spring, he dons a brighter coat of tawny-red and along his sides, where the red meets the grayish white of the under side, there is a dark line which is very ornamental; and now his tail is a shower of ruddiness. As the season advances, the colors seem to fade; they are probably a part of his wooing costume. When dashing up a tree trunk, his color is never very striking but looks like the glimmer of sunlight; this has probably saved many of his kind from the gunner, whose eyes being at the front of his head, cannot compare in efficiency with those of the squirrel, which being large and full and alert, are placed at the sides of the head so as to see equally well in all directions.

The squirrel's legs are short because he is essentially a climber rather than a runner; the hips are very strong, which insures his power as a jumper, and his leaps are truly remarkable. A squirrel uses his front paws for hands in a most human way; with them he washes his face and holds his food up to his mouth while eating, and it is interesting

Squirrel Tracks

to note the skill of his claws when used as fingers. The track he makes in the snow is quite characteristic. The tracks are paired and those of the large five-toed hind feet are always in front.

The squirrel has two pairs of gnawing teeth which are very long and strong, as in all rodents, and he needs to keep busy gnawing hard things with them, or they will grow so long that he cannot use them at all and will starve to death. He is very clever about opening nuts so as to get all the meats. He often opens a hickory nut with two holes which tap the places of the nut meats squarely; with walnuts or butternuts, which have much harder shells, he makes four small holes, one opposite each quarter of the kernel. He has no cheek-pouches like a chipmunk but he can carry corn and other grain. He often fills his mouth so full that his cheeks bulge out like those of a boy eating popcorn; but anything as large as a nut he carries in his teeth. His food is far more varied than many suppose and he will eat almost anything eatable; he is a little pirate and enjoys stealing from others with keenest zest. In spring, he eats leaf buds and hunts our orchards for apple seeds. In winter, he feeds on nuts and cones; it is marvelous how he will take a cone apart, tearing off the scales and leaving them in a heap while searching for seeds; he is especially fond of the seeds of Norway spruce and hemlock. Of course, he is fond of nuts of all kinds and will cut the chestnut burs from the tree before they are ripe, so that he may get ahead of the other harvesters. He stores his food for winter in all sorts of odd places and often forgets where he puts it. We often find his winter stores untouched the next summer. He also likes birds' eggs and nestlings, and if it were not for the chastisement he gets from the parent

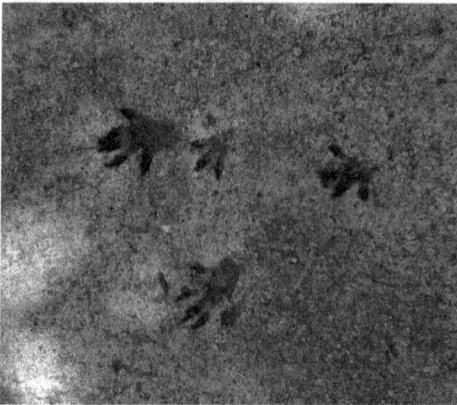
A squirrel hop preserved in concrete

Close-up of an eastern gray squirrel's head; note the brownish fur on its face, the gray fur on its back and the white fur on its underside.

robins, he would work much damage in this way.

The squirrel is likely to be a luxurious fellow and have a winter and a summer home. The former is in some hollow tree or other protected place; the summer home consists of a platform of twigs in some tree-top, often built upon an abandoned crow or hawk nest; but just how he uses these two homes, is as yet, a matter of guessing and is a good subject for young naturalists to investigate. During the winter, he does not remain at home except in coldest weather, when he lies cozily with his tail wrapped around him like a boa to keep him warm. He is too full of interest in the world to lie quietly long, but comes out, hunts up some of his stores, and finds life worth while despite the cold. One squirrel adopted a bird house in one of our trees, and he or his kin have lived there for years; in winter, he takes his share of the suet put on the trees for birds, and because of his greediness, we have been compelled to use picture wire for tying on the suet.

The young are born in a protected nest, usually in the hollow of a tree. There are four to six young in a litter and they appear in April. If necessary to move the young, the mother carries the squirrel baby clinging to her breast with its arms around her neck.

The squirrel has several ways of expressing his emotions; one is by various curves in his long beautiful, bushy tail. If the creatures of the wood had a stage, the squirrel would have to be their chief actor. Surprise, incredulousness, indignation, fear, anger and joy are all perfectly expressed by tail gestures and also by voice. As a vocalist he excels; he chatters with curiosity, "chips" with surprise, scolds by giving a gutteral trill, finishing with a falsetto squeal. He is the only singer I know who can carry two parts at a time. Notice him sometimes in the top of a hickory or chestnut tree when nuts are ripe, and you will hear him singing a duet all by himself, a high shrill chatter with a chuckling accompaniment. Long may he abide with us as an uninvited guest at our cribs! For, though he be a freebooter and conscienceless, yet our world would lack its highest example of incarnate grace and activity, if he were not in it.

LESSON

Leading Thought— The red squirrel by its agility and cleverness has lived on,

Flying squirrel at a feeder

despite its worst enemy—man. By form and color and activity it is fitted to elude the hunter.

Method— If a pet squirrel in a cage can be procured for observation at the school, the observations on the form and habits of the animal can be best studied thus; but a squirrel in a cage is an anomaly and it is far better to stimulate the pupils to observe the squirrels out of doors. Give the following questions, a few at a time, and ask the pupils to report the answers to the entire class. Much should be done with the supplementary reading, as there are many interesting squirrel stories illustrating its habits.

Observations—

1. Where have you seen a squirrel? Does the squirrel trot along or

leap when running on the ground? Does it run straight ahead or stop at intervals for observation? How does it look? How does it act when looking to see if the "coast is clear"?

2. When climbing a tree, does it go straight up, or move around the trunk? How does it hide itself behind a tree trunk and observe the passer-by? Describe how it manages to climb a tree. Does it go down the tree head first? Is it able to climb out on the smallest branches? Of what advantage is this to it?

3. Look closely and see if a squirrel follows the same route always when passing from one point to another. How does it pass from tree to tree? How does it act when preparing to jump? How does it hold its legs and tail when in the air during a jump from branch to branch?

4. Describe the colors of the red squirrel above and below. Is there a dark stripe along its side, if so, what color? How does the color of the squirrel protect it from its enemies? Is its color brighter in summer or in winter?

5. How are the squirrel's eyes placed? Do you think it can see behind as well as in front all the time? Are its eyes bright and alert, or soft and tender?

6. Are its legs long or short? Are its hind legs stronger and longer than the front legs? Why? Why does it not need long legs? Does its paws have claws? How does it use its paws when eating and in making its toilet?

7. Describe the squirrel's tail. Is it as long as the body? Is it used to express emotion? Of what use is it when the squirrel is jumping? Of what use is it in the winter in the nest?

8. What is the food of the squirrel during the autumn? Winter? Spring? Summer? Where does it store food for the winter? Does it steal food laid up by jays, chipmunks, mice or other squirrels? How does it carry nuts? Has it cheek-pouches like the chipmunk for carrying food? Does it stay in its nest all winter living on stored food like a chipmunk?

9. Where does the red squirrel make its winter home? Does it also have a summer home, if so, of what is it made and where built? In what sort of a nest are the young born and reared? At what time of the year are the young born? How does the mother squirrel carry her little ones if she wishes to move them?

Western gray squirrel

10. How much of squirrel language can you understand? How does it express surprise, excitement, anger, or joy during the nut harvest? Note how many different sounds it makes and try to discover what they mean.

11. Describe or sketch the tracks made by the squirrel in the snow.

12. How does the squirrel get at the meats of the hickory nut and the walnut? How are its teeth arranged to gnaw holes in such hard substances as shells?

Supplementary Reading— Squirrels and Other Fur-Bearers, John Burroughs; *American Animals, Stone & Cram*; Secrets of the Woods, Long; *Familiar Life in Field and Forest*, Mathews; *Little Beasts of Field and Wood*, Cram; *Wild Neighbors*, Ingersoll; *Familiar Wild Animals*, Lottridge.

Furry

FURRY was a baby red squirrel. One day in May his mother was moving him from one tree to another. He was clinging with his little arms around her neck and his body clasped tightly against her breast, when something frightened her and in her sudden movement, she dropped her heavy baby in the grass. Thus, I inherited him and entered upon the rather onerous duties of caring for a baby of whose needs I knew little; but I knew that every well cared for baby should have a book detailing all that happens to it, therefore, I made a book for Furry, writing in it each day the things he did. If the children who have pets keep similar books, they will find them most interesting reading afterward, and they will surely enjoy the writing very much.

EXTRACTS FROM FURRY'S NOTE-BOOK

MAY 18, 1902—The baby squirrel is just large enough to cuddle in one hand. He cuddles all right when once he is captured; but he is a terrible fighter, and when I attempt to take him in my hand, he scratches and bites and growls so that I have been obliged to name him Fury. I told him, however, if he improved in temper I would change his name to Furry.

MAY 19—Fury greets me, when I open his box, with the most awe-inspiring little growls, which he calculates will make me turn pale with fear. He has not cut his teeth yet, so he cannot bite very severely, but that isn't his fault, for he tries hard enough. The Naturalist said cold milk would kill him, so I warmed the milk and put it in a teaspoon and placed it in front of his nose; he batted the spoon with both forepaws and tried to bite it, and thus got a taste of the milk, which he drank eagerly, lapping it up like a kitten. When I hold him in one hand and cover him with the other, he turns contented little somersaults over and over.

MAY 20—Fury bit me only once to-day, when I took him out to feed him. He is cutting his teeth on my devoted fingers. I tried giving him grape-nuts soaked in milk, but he spat it out in disgust. Evidently he does not believe he needs a food for brain and nerve. He always washes his face as soon as he is through eating.

MAY 21—Fury lies curled up under his blanket all day. Evidently good little squirrels stay quietly in the nest, when the mother is not at home to give them permission to run around. When Fury sleeps, he rolls himself up in a little ball with his tail wrapped closely around him. The squirrel's tail is his "furs," which he wraps around him to keep his back warm when he sleeps in winter.

MAY 23—Every time I meet Uncle John he asks, "Is his name Fury or Furry now?" Uncle John is much interested in the good behavior of even little squirrels. As Fury has not bitten me hard for two days, I think I will call him Furry after this. He ate some bread soaked in milk to-day, holding it in his hands in real squirrel fashion. I let him run around the room and he liked it.

MAY 25—Furry got away from me this morning and I did not find him for an hour. Then I discovered him in a pasteboard box of drawing paper with the cover on. How did he squeeze through?

May 26—He holds the bowl of the spoon with both front paws while he drinks the milk. When I try to draw the spoon away, to fill it again after he has emptied it, he objects and hangs on to it with all his little might, and scolds as hard as ever he can. He is such a funny, unreasonable baby.

MAY 28—To-night I gave Furry a walnut meat. As soon as he smelled it he became greatly excited; he grasped the meat in his hands and ran off and hid under my elbow, growling like a kitten with its first mouse.

MAY 30—Since he tasted nuts he has lost interest in milk. The nut meats are too hard for his new teeth, so I mash them and soak them in water and now he eats them like a little piggy-wig with no manners at all. He loves to have me stroke his back while he is eating. He uses his thumbs and fingers in such a human way that I always call his front paws *hands.* When his piece of nut is very small he holds it in one hand and clasps the other hand behind the one which holds the dainty morsel, so as to keep it safe.

MAY 31—When he is sleepy he scolds if I disturb him and, turning over on his back, bats my hand with all of his soft little paws and pretends that he is going to bite.

JUNE 4—Furry ranges around the room now to please himself. He is a little mischief; he tips over his cup of milk and has commenced gnawing off the wall paper behind the book-shelf to make him a nest. The paper is green and will probably make him sorry.

JUNE 5—This morning Furry was hidden in a roll of paper. I put my hand over one end of the roll and then reached in with the other hand to get him; but he got me instead, because he ran up my sleeve and was much more contented to be there than I was to have him. I was glad enough when he left his hiding place and climbed to the top shelf of the bookcase, far beyond my reach.

JUNE 6—I have not seen Furry for twenty-four hours, but he is here surely enough. Last night he tipped over the ink bottle and scattered nut shells over the floor. He prefers pecans to any other nuts.

JUNE 7—I caught Furry to-day and he bit my finger so it bled. But afterwards, he cuddled in my hand for a long time, and then climbed my shoulder and went hunting around in my hair and wanted to stay there and make a nest. When I took him away, he pulled out his two hands full of my devoted tresses. I'll not employ him as a hairdresser.

JUNE 9—Furry sleeps nights in the top drawer of my desk; he crawls in from behind. When I pull out the drawer he pops out and scares me nearly out of my wits; but he keeps his wits about him and gets away before I can catch him.

JUNE 20—I keep the window open so Furry can run out and in and learn to take care of himself out-of-doors.

Furry soon learned to take care of himself, though he often returned for nuts, which I kept for him in a bowl. He does not come very near me out-of-doors, but he often speaks to me in a friendly manner from a certain pitch pine tree near the house.

There are many blank leaves in Furry's note-book. I wish that he could have written on these of the things that he thought about me and my performances. It would certainly have been the most interesting book concerning squirrels in the world.

The Chipmunk

HILE the chipmunk is a good runner and jumper, it is not so able a climber as is the red squirrel, and it naturally stays nearer the ground. One windy day I was struck by the peculiar attitude of what, I first thought, was a red squirrel gathering green acorns from a chestnut oak in front of my window. A second glance showed me that it was a chipmunk lying close to the branch, hanging on for "dear life" and with an attitude of extreme caution, quite foreign to the red squirrel in a similar situation. He would creep out, seize an acorn in its teeth, creep back to a larger limb, take off the shell, and with his little paws stuff the kernel into his cheek pouches; he took hold of one side of his mouth with one hand to stretch it out, as if opening a bag, and stuffed the acorn in with the other. I do not know whether this process was necessary or not at the beginning, for his cheeks were distended when I first saw him;

and he kept on stuffing them until he looked as if he had a hopeless case of mumps. Then with obvious care he descended the tree and retreated to his den in the side hill, the door of which I had already discovered, although it was well hidden by a bunch of orchard grass.

Allen's chipmunk

Chipmunks are more easily tamed than red squirrels and soon learn that pockets may contain nuts and other things good to eat. The first tame chipmunk of my acquaintance belonged to a species found in the California mountains. He was a beautiful little creature and loved to play about his mistress' room; she, being a naturalist as well as a poet, was able to understand her little companion, and the relations between them were full of mutual confidence. He was fond of English walnuts and would always hide away all that were placed in a dish on the table. One day his mistress, when taking off her bonnet after returning from church, discovered several of these nuts tucked safely in the velvet bows; they were invisible from the front but perfectly visible from the side. Even yet, she wonders what the people at church that day thought of her original ideas in millinery; and she wonders still more how "Chipsie" managed to get into the bonnet-box, the cover of which was always carefully closed.

The chipmunk is a good home builder and carries off, presumably in its cheek pouches, all of the soil which it removes in making its burrow. The burrow is made usually in a dry hillside, the passageway just

Chipmunk hibernating

large enough for its own body, widening to a nest which is well bedded down. There is usually a back door also, so that in case of necessity, the inmate can escape. It retires to this nest in late November and does not appear again until March. In the nest, it stores nuts and other grains so that when it wakens, at long intervals, it can take refreshment.

If you really wish to know whether you see what you look at or not, test yourself by trying to describe the length, position and number of the chipmunk's stripes. These stripes, like those of the tiger in the jungle, make the creature less conspicuous; when on the ground, where its stripes fall in with the general shape and color of the grass and underbrush, it is quite invisible until it stirs. Its tail is not so long nor nearly so bushy as that of the squirrel; it does not need a tail to balance and steer with in the tree tops; and since it lives in the ground, a bushy tail would soon be loaded with earth and would be an incubus instead of a thing of beauty.

The chipmunk is not a vocalist like the red squirrel, but he can cluck like a cuckoo and chatter gayly or cogently; and he can make himself into a little bunch with his tail curved up his back, while he eats a nut from both his hands, and is even more amusing than the red squirrel in this attitude; probably because he is more innocent and not so much of a *poseur.* His food consists of all kinds of nuts, grain and fruit, but he does little or no damage, as a rule. He is pretty and distinctly companionable, and I can rejoice, in that I have had him and his whole family as my near neighbors for many years. I always feel especially proud when he shows his confidence, by scampering around our piazza floor and peeping in at our windows, as if taking a reciprocal interest in us.

LESSON

Leading thought— The chipmunk lives more on the ground than does the squirrel; its colors are protective and it has cheek pouches in which it carries food, and also soil when digging its burrow. It stores food for winter in its den.

Method— The field note-book should be the basis for this work. Give the pupils an outline of observations to be made, and ask for reports now and then. Meanwhile stimulate interest in the little creatures by reading aloud from some of the references given.

Observations—

1. Do you see the chipmunk climbing around in trees like the red squirrel? How high in a tree have you ever seen a chipmunk?

2. What are the chipmunk's colors above and below? How many stripes has it? Where are they and what are their colors? Do you think that these stripes conceal the animal when among grasses and bushes?

3. Compare the tails of the chipmunk and the red squirrel. Which is the longer and bushier? Tell if you can the special advantage to the chipmunk in having this less bushy tail?

4. What does the chipmunk eat? How does it carry its food? How does it differ in this respect from the red squirrel? Does it store its food for winter use? How does it prepare its nuts? How does it hold its food while eating?

5. Where does the chipmunk make its home? How does it carry away soil from its burrow? How many entrances are there? How is the den arranged inside? Does it live in the same den the year round?

An eastern chipmunk placing food in its cheek pouch

When does it retire to its den in the fall? When does it come out in the spring?

6. Does the chipmunk do any damage to crops? What seeds does it distribute? At what time do the little chipmunks appear in the spring?

7. Observe carefully the different tones of the chipmunk and compare its chattering with that of the squirrel.

Supplementary reading— Squirrels and Other Fur-Bearers, John Burroughs; *American Animals,* Stone and Cram.

TO A CAPTIVE CHIPMUNK OF THE SIERRAS

Bright little comrade from the woods, come show
Thy antic cheer about my sunlit room
Of books, that stand in moods of gloom
Because thought's tide is out, heart's rhythm is low
With weariness. Friendly thou art and know
Good friend in me, who yet did dare presume
To take thee from thy home, thy little doom
To make for thee, and longer life bestow.
So, thou hast not been eaten by the snake;
Thy gentle blood no weasel drank at night;
Thou hast not starved 'mid winter's frozen wood,
Nor waited vainly for the sun to make
Sweet the wild nuts for thee. Yet, little sprite,
Thou still doth question if my deed were good?

—*Irene Hardy*

A bat

The Little Brown Bat

TEACHER'S STORY

His small umbrella, quaintly halved,
Describing in the air an arc alike inscrutable,—
Elate philosopher!

—EMILY DICKINSON

HOEVER first said "as blind as a bat," surely never looked a bat in the face, or he would not have said it. The deep-set, keen, observant eyes are quite in keeping with the alert attitude of the erect, pointed ears; while the pug-nose and the wide open, little, pink bag of a mouth, set with tiny, sharp teeth, give this anomalous little animal a deliciously impish look. Yet how have those old artists belied the bat, who fashioned their demons after his pattern, ears, eyes, nose, mouth, wings and all! Certain it is, if human beings ever get to be winged angels in this world, they are far more likely to have their wings fashioned like those of the bat than like those of the bird. As a matter of fact, there are no other wings so wonderful as the bat's; the thin membrane is equipped with sensitive nerves which inform the flier of the objects in his path, so that he darts among the branches of trees at terrific speed and never touches a twig; a blinded bat was once set free in a room, across which threads were stretched, and he flew about without ever touching one. After we have tamed one of these little, silky flittermice we soon get reconciled to his wings for he proves the cunningest of pets; he soon learns who feeds him, and is a constant source of entertainment.

The flight of the bat is the highest ideal we may have, for the achievement of the aeroplane. It consists of darting hither and thither with incredible swiftness, and making sharp turns with no apparent effort.

Little brown bat during winter hibernation

Swifts and swallows are the only birds that can compete with the bat in wing celerity and agility; it is interesting to note that these birds also catch insects on the wing, for food. The bat, like the swift, keeps his mouth open, scooping in all the insects in his way; more than this, he makes a collecting net of the wing membrane, stretched between the hind legs and tail, doubling it up like an apron on the unfortunate insects, and then reaching down and gobbling them up; and thus he is always doing good service to us on summer evenings by swallowing mosquitoes and gnats.

The short fur of the bat is as soft as silk, and covers the body but not the wings; the plan of the wing is something like that of the duck's foot; it consists of a web stretched between very much elongated fingers. If a boy's fingers were as long, in proportion, as a bat's, they would measure four feet. Stretched between the long fingers is a thin, rubbery membrane, which extends back to the ankles and thence back to the tip of the bony tail; thus, the bat has a winged margin all around his body. Since fingers make the framework, it is the thumb that projects from the front angle of the wing, in the form of a very serviceable hook, resembling that used by a one-armed man to replace the lost member. These hooks the bat uses in many

The face of a little brown bat

ways. He drags himself along the floor with their aid, or he scratches the back of his head with them, if occasion requires. He is essentially a creature of the air and is not at all fitted for walking; his knees bend backward in an opposite direction from ours. This renders him unable to walk, and when attempting to do so, he has the appearance of "scrabbling" along on his feet and elbows. When thus moving he keeps his wings fluttering rapidly, as if feeling his way in the dark, and his movements are trembly. He uses his teeth to aid in climbing.

The little brown bat's wings often measure nine inches from tip to tip, and yet he folds them so that they scarcely show; he does not fold them like a fan, but rather like a pocket knife. The hind legs merely act as a support for the side wing, and the little hip bones look pitifully sharp; the membrane reaches only to the ankle, the tiny emaciated foot projecting from it is armed with five, wirelike toes, tipped with sharp hooked claws. It is by these claws that he hangs when resting during the day, for he is upside-down-y in his sleeping habits, slumbering during the daytime, while hanging head downward, without any inconvenience from a rush of blood to the brain; when thus suspended, the tail is folded down. Sometimes he hangs by one hind foot and a front hook; and he is a wee thing when all folded together and hung up, with his nose tucked between his hooked thumbs, in a very babyish fashion.

The bat is very particular about his personal cleanliness. People who regard the bat as a dirty creature, had better look to it that they are even half as fastidious as he. He washes his face with the front

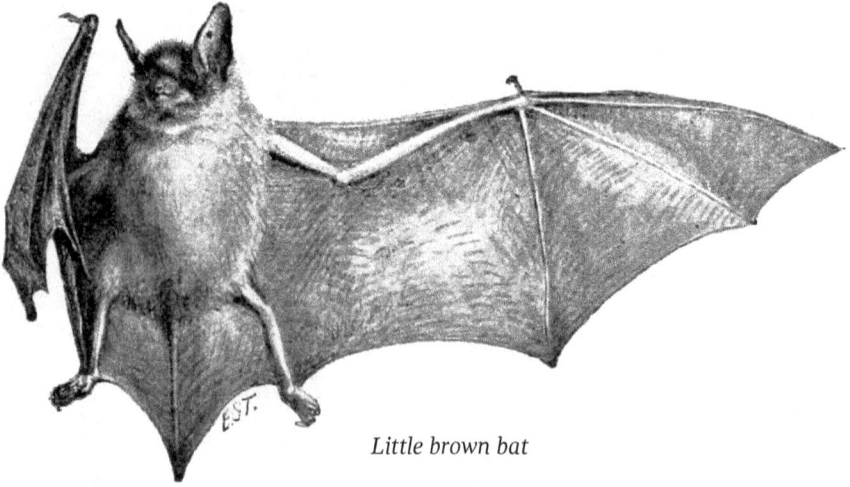
Little brown bat

part of his wing, and then licks his wash-cloth clean; he scratches the back of his head with his hind foot and then licks the foot; when hanging head down, he will reach one hind foot down and scratch behind his ear with an *aplomb* truly comical in such a mite; but it is most fun of all to see him clean his wings; he seizes the edges in his mouth and stretches and licks the membrane until we are sure it is made of silk elastic, for he pulls and hauls it in a way truly amazing.

The bat has a voice which sounds like the squeak of a toy wheelbarrow, and yet it is expressive of emotions. He squeaks in one tone when holding conversation with other bats, and squeaks quite differently when seized by the enemy.

The mother bat feeds her little ones from her breasts as a mouse does its young, only she cradles them in her soft wings while so doing; often she takes them with her when she goes out for insects in the evenings; they cling to her neck during these exciting rides; but when she wishes to work unencumbered, she hangs her tiny youngsters on some twig and goes back to them later. The little ones are born in July and usually occur as twins. During the winter, bats hibernate like woodchucks or chipmunks. They select for winter quarters some hollow tree or cave or other protected place. They go to sleep when the cold weather comes, and do not awake until the insects are flying; they then come forth in the evenings, or perhaps early in the morning, and do their best to rid the world of mosquitoes and other insect nuisances.

There are many senseless fears about the bat; for instance, that he likes to get tangled in a lady's tresses, a situation which would frighten him far more than the lady; or that he brings bedbugs into the house, when he enters on his quest for mosquitoes, which is an ungrateful slander. Some people believe that all bats are vampires, and only await an opportunity to suck blood from their victims. It is true that in South America

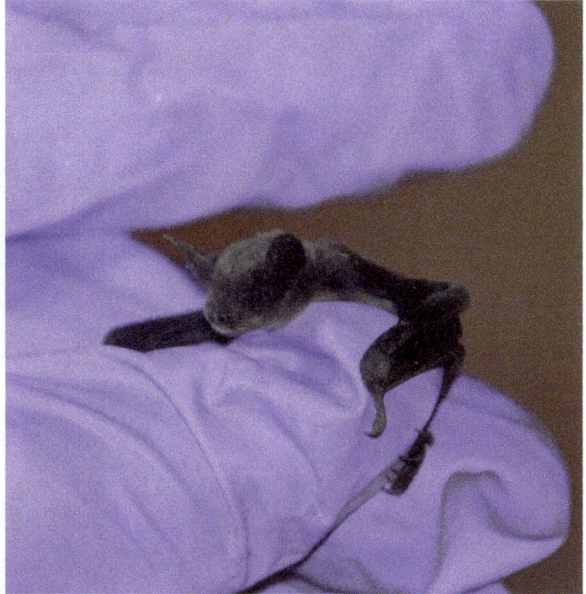
A newborn little brown bat

there are two species which occasionally attack people who are careless enough to sleep with their toes uncovered, but feet thus injured seem to recover speedily; and these bats do little damage to people, although they sometimes pester animals; but there are no vampires in the United States. Our bats, on the contrary, are innocent and beneficial to man; and if we had more of them we should have less malaria. There a few species in our country, which have little, leaf-like growths on the end of the nose; and when scientists study the bat from a nature-study instead of an anatomical standpoint, we shall know what these leafy appendages are used for.

LESSON

Leading thought— Although the bat's wings are very different from those of the bird's yet it is a rapid and agile flier. It flies in the dusk and catches great numbers of mosquitoes and other troublesome insects, upon which it feeds.

Method— This lesson should not be given unless there is a live bat to illustrate it; the little creature can be cared for comfortably in a cage

A bat colony

in the schoolroom, as it will soon learn to take flies or bits of raw meat when presented on the point of a pencil or toothpick. Any bat will do for this study, although the little brown bat is the one on which my observations were made.

Observations—

1. At what time of day do we see bats flying? Describe how the bat's flight differs from that of birds. Why do bats dart about so rapidly?

2. Look at a captive bat and describe its wings. Can you see what makes the framework of the wings? Do you see the three finger bones extending out into the wings? How do the hind legs support the wing? The tail? Is the wing membrane covered with fur? Is it thick and leathery or thin and silky and elastic? How does the bat fold up its wings?

3. In what position does the bat rest? Does it ever hang by its thumb hooks?

4. Can you see whether the knees of the hind legs bend upward or downward? How does the bat act when trying to walk or crawl? How does it use its thumb hooks in doing this?

5. What does the bat do daytimes? Where does it stay during the day? Do many bats congregate together in their roosts?

6. Describe the bat's head, including the ears, eyes, nose and mouth. What is its general expression? Do you think it can see and hear well? How is its mouth fitted for catching insects? Does it shut its mouth while chewing or keep it open? Do you think that bats can see by daylight?

7. What noises does a bat make? How does it act if you try to touch it? Can it bite severely? Can you understand why the Germans call it a flitter-mouse?

8. Do you know how the mother bat cares for her young? How does she carry them? At what time of year may we expect to find them?

9. When making its toilet, how does a bat clean its wings? Its face? Its back? Its feet? Do you know if it is very clean in its habits?

10. How and where do the bats pass the winter? How are they beneficial to us? Are they ever harmful?

Supplementary reading— American Animals, Stone and Cram.

Nature-study should not be unrelated to the child's life and circumstances. It stands for directness and naturalness. It is astonishing when one comes to think of it, how indirect and how remote from the lives of pupils much of our education has been. Geography still often begins with the universe, and finally, perhaps, comes down to some concrete and familiar object or scene that the pupil can understand. Arithmetic has to do with brokerage and partnerships and partial payments and other things that mean nothing to the child. Botany begins with cells and protoplasm and cryptogams. History deals with political and military affairs, and only rarely comes down to physical facts and to those events that express the real lives of the people; and yet political and social affairs are only the results of expressions of the way in which people live. Readers begin with mere literature or with stories of scenes the child will never see. Of course these statements are meant to be only general, as illustrating what is even yet a great fault in educational methods. There are many exceptions, and these are becoming commoner. Surely, the best education is that which begins with the materials at hand. A child knows a stone before it knows the earth.

—L. H. BAILEY "THE NATURE-STUDY IDEA"

The Skunk

HOSE who have had experience with this animal, surely are glad that it is small; and the wonder always is, that so little a creature can make such a large impression upon the atmosphere. A fully grown skunk is about two feet long; its body is covered with long, shining, rather coarse hair, and the tail, which is carried like a flag in the air, is very large and bushy. In color, the fur is sometimes entirely black, but most often has a white patch on the back of the neck, with two stripes extending down the back and along the sides to the tail; the face, also, has a white stripe.

The skunk has a long head and a rather pointed snout; its front legs are very much shorter than its hind legs, which gives it a very peculiar gait. Its forefeet are armed with long, strong claws, with which it digs its burrow, which is usually made in light soil. It also often makes its home in some crevice in rocks, or even takes possession of an aban-

60

doned woodchuck's hole; or trusting to its immunity from danger, makes its home under the barn. In the fall, it becomes very fat, and during the early part of winter, hibernates within its den; it comes out during the thaws of winter and early spring.

The young skunks appear in May; they are born in an enlarged portion of the burrow, where a nice bed of grass and leaves is made for them; the skunk is scrupulously neat about its own nest. The young skunks are very active, and interesting to watch, when playing together like kittens.

The skunk belongs to the same family as the mink and weasel, which also give off a disagreeable odor when angry. The fetid material, which is the skunk's defence, is contained in two capsules under the root of the tail. These little capsules are not larger than peas, and the quantity of liquid forced from them in a discharge is scarcely more than a large drop; yet it will permeate the atmosphere with its odor for a distance of a mile. The fact that this discharge is so disagreeable to all other animals, has had a retarding influence upon the skunk's intelligence. It has not been obliged to rely upon its cunning to escape its enemies, and has therefore never developed either fear or cleverness. It marches abroad without haste, confident that every creature which sees it will give it plenty of room. It is a night prowler, although it is not averse to a daytime promenade. The white upon its fur gives warning at night, that here is an animal which had best be left alone. This immunity from attack makes the skunk careless in learning wisdom from experience; it never learns to avoid a trap or a railway or trolley track.

The skunk's food consists largely of insects, mice, snakes and other small animals. It also destroys the eggs and young of birds which nest upon the ground. It uses its strong forepaws in securing its prey. Dr. Merriam, who made pets of young skunks after removing their scent capsules, found them very interesting. He says of one which was named "Meph": "We used to walk through the woods to a large meadow that abounded in grasshoppers. Here, Meph would fairly revel in his favorite food, and it was rich sport to watch his manoeuvres. When a grasshopper jumped, he jumped, and I have seen him with as many as three in his mouth and two under his fore-paws at the same time."

A striped skunk. Note the long, pointed head and the bushy tail

The only injury which the skunk is likely to do to the farmers, is the raiding of the hens' nests, and this can be obviated by properly housing the poultry. On the other hand, the skunk is of great use in destroying injurious insects and mice. Often when skunks burrow beneath barns, they completely rid the place of mice. Skunk fur is very valuable and is sold under the name of Alaskan sable. The skunk takes short steps, and goes so slowly that it makes a double track, the imprints being very close together. The foot makes a longer track than that of the cat, as the skunk is plantigrade; that is, it walks upon its palms and heels as well as its toes.

References— Wild Neighbors, Ingersoll; Familiar Life in Field and Forest, Mathews; American Animals, Stone and Cram; Squirrels and Other Fur-Bearers, Burroughs.

Skunk Tracks

LESSON

Leading thought— The skunk has depended so long upon protecting itself from its enemies by its disagreeable odor, that it has become stupid in this respect, and seems never to be able to learn to keep off of railroad tracks. It is a very beneficial animal to the farmer because its food consists so largely of injurious insects and rodents.

Method— The questions should be given the pupils and they should answer them from personal observations or inquiries.

Observations—

1. How large is a skunk? Describe its fur. Where does the black and white occur in the fur? Of what use is the white to the skunk? Is the fur valuable? What is its commercial name?

2. What is the shape of the skunk's head? The general shape of the body? The tail? Are the front legs longer or shorter than the hind legs? Describe the front feet. For what are they used?

3. Where and how does the skunk make its nest? Does it sleep like a woodchuck during the winter? What is its food? How does it catch its prey? Does it hunt for its food during the day or the night? Does the skunk ever hurry? Is it afraid? How does it protect itself from its enemies? Do you think that the skunk's freedom from fear has rendered the animal less intelligent?

4. At what time do the skunk kittens appear? Have you ever seen little skunks playing? If so, describe their antics. How is the nest made soft for the young ones?

5. How does the skunk benefit farmers? Does it ever do them any injury? Do you think that it does more good than harm?

6. Describe the skunk's track as follows: How many toes show in the track? Does the palm or heel show? Are the tracks near together? Do they form a single or a double line?

Supplementary reading— *Squirrels and Other Fur-Bearers*, Burroughs.

Saw a little skunk coming up the river bank in the woods at the white oak, a funny little fellow, about six inches long and nearly as broad. It faced me and actually compelled me to retreat before it for five minutes. Perhaps I was between it and its hole. Its broad black tail, tipped with white, was erect like a kitten's. It had what looked like a broad white band drawn tight across its forehead or top-head, from which two lines of white ran down, one on each side of its back, and there was a narrow white line down its snout. It raised its back, sometimes ran a few feet forward, sometimes backward, and repeatedly turned its tail to me, prepared to discharge its fluid, like the old ones. Such was its instinct, and all the while it kept up a fine grunting like a little pig or a red squirrel.

—HENRY THOREAU

Few animals are so silent as the skunk. Zoological works contain no information as to its voice, and the essayists rarely mention it except by implication. Mr. Burroughs says: "The most silent creature known to me, he makes no sound, so far as I have observed, save a diffuse, impatient noise, like that produced by beating your hand with a whisk-broom, when the farm-dog has discovered his retreat in the stone fence." Rowland Robinson tells us that: "The voiceless creature sometimes frightens the belated farm-boy, whom he curiously follows with a mysterious hollow beating of his feet upon the ground." Thoreau, as has been mentioned, heard one keep up a "fine grunting, like a little pig or a squirrel;" but he seems to have misunderstood altogether a singular loud patting sound heard repeatedly on the frozen ground under the wall, which he also listened to, for he thought it "had to do with getting its food, patting the earth to get the insects or worms." Probably he would have omitted this guess if he could have edited his diary instead of leaving that to be done after his death. The patting is evidently merely a nervous sign of impatience or apprehension, similar to the well-known stamping with the hind feet indulged in by rabbits, in this case probably a menace like a doubling of the fists, as the hind legs, with which they kick, are their only weapons. The skunk, then, is not voiceless, but its voice is weak and querulous, and it is rarely if ever heard except in the expression of anger.

—ERNEST INGERSOLL IN "WILD NEIGHBORS"

The Raccoon

ONE other of our little brothers of the forest, has such a mischievous countenance as the coon. The black patch across the face and surrounding the eyes, like large goggles, and the black line extending from the long, inquisitive nose directly up the forehead give the coon's face an anxious expression; and the keenness of the big, beady, black eyes and the alert, "sassy" looking, broadly triangular ears, convince one that the anxiety depicted in the face is anxiety lest something that should *not* be done be left undone; and I am sure that anyone who has had experience with pet coons will aver that their acts do not belie their looks.

What country child, wandering by the brook and watching its turbulence in early spring, has not viewed with awe, a footprint on the muddy banks looking as if it were made by the foot of a very little baby. The first one I ever saw, I promptly concluded was made by the foot of

Raccoon Tracks
1. Walking 2. Jumping

a brook fairy. However, the coon is no fairy; it is a rather heavy, logy animal and, like the bear and skunk, is plantigrade, walking on the entire foot instead of on the toes, like a cat or dog. The hind foot is long, with a well-marked heel, and five comparatively short toes, giving it a remarkable resemblance to a human foot. The front foot is smaller and looks like a wide, little hand, with four long fingers and a rather short thumb. The claws are strong and sharp. The soles of the feet and the palms of the hands look as if they were covered with black kid, while the feet above and the backs of the hands are covered with short fur. Coon tracks are likely to be found during the first thawing days of winter, along some stream or the borders of swamps, often following the path made by cattle. The full-length track is about 2 inches long; as the coon puts the hind foot in the track made by the front foot on the same side, only the print of the hind feet is left, showing plainly five toe prints and the heel. The tracks may vary from one-half inch to one foot or more apart, depending on how fast the animal is going; when it runs it goes on its toes, but when walking sets the heel down; the tracks are not in so straight a line as those made by the cat. Sometimes it goes at a slow jump, when the prints of the hind feet are paired, and between and behind them are the prints of the two front feet.

The coon is covered with long, rather coarse hair, so long as to almost drag when the animal is walking; it really has two different kinds of hair, the long, coarse, gray hair, blackened at the tips, covering the fine, short, grayish or brownish under coat. The very handsome bushy tail is ringed with black and gray.

The raccoon feeds on almost anything eatable, except herbage. It has a special predilection for corn in the milk stage and, in attaining this sweet and toothsome luxury, it strips down the husks and often breaks the plant, doing much damage. It is also fond of poultry and often raids hen houses; it also destroys birds' nests and the young, thus damaging the farmer by killing both domestic and wild birds. It is especially fond of fish and is an adept at sitting on the shore and catching them with its hands; it likes turtle eggs, crayfish and snakes; it haunts the bayous of the Gulf Coast for the oysters which grow there; it is

A raccoon in a tree

also a skillful frog catcher. Although fond of animal diet, it is also fond of fruit, especially of berries and wild grapes.

It usually chooses for a nest a hollow tree or a cavern in a ledge near a stream, because of its liking for water creatures; and also because of its strange habit of washing its meat before eating it. I have watched a pet coon performing this act; he would take a piece of meat in his hands, dump it into the pan of drinking water and souse it up and down a few times; then he would get into the pan with his splay feet and roll the meat beneath and between them, meanwhile looking quite unconcernedly at his surroundings, as if washing the meat were an act too mechanical to occupy his mind. After the meat had become soaked until white and flabby, he would take it in his hands and hang on to it with a tight grip while he pulled off pieces with his teeth; or sometimes he would hold it with his feet, and use hands as well as teeth in tearing it apart. The coon's teeth are very much like those of the cat, having long, sharp tushes or canines, and sharp, wedge-shaped grinding teeth, which cut as well as grind. After eating, the pet coon always washed his feet by splashing them in the pan.

It is a funny sight to watch a coon arrange itself for a nap, on a branch or in the fork of a tree; it adapts its fat body to the unevenness of the bed with apparent comfort; it then tucks its nose down between its paws and curls its tail about itself, making a huge, furry ball. In all probability, the rings of gray and black on the tail, serve as protective color to the animal sleeping in a tree during the daytime, when sunshine and shadow glance down between the leaves with ever-changing light. The coon spends much of its days asleep in some such situation, and comes forth at night to seek its food.

In the fall, the coon lays on fat enough to last it during its winter sleep. Usually several inhabit the same nest in winter, lying curled up together in a hollow tree, and remaining dormant all winter except when awakened by the warmth of a thaw. They then may come forth to see what is happening, but return shortly to wait until March or April; then they issue to hunt for the scant food, and are so lean and weak that they fall easy prey to their enemies.

The young are born in April and May; there are from three to six in a litter; they are blind and helpless at first, and are cared for carefully by their parents, the family remaining together for a year, until the young are fully grown. If removed from their parents the young ones cry pitifully, almost like babies. The cry or whistle of the fully grown coon is anything but a happy sound, and is quite impossible to describe. I have been awakened by it many a night in camp, and it always sounded strange, taking on each time new quavers and whimperings. As a cry, it is first cousin to that of the screech-owl.

The stories of pet coons are many. I knew one which, chained in a yard, would lie curled up near its post looking like an innocent stone except for one eye kept watchfully open. Soon a hen, filled with curiosity, would come warily near, looking longingly at remains of food in the pan; the coon made no move until the disarmed biddy came close to the pan. Then, there was a scramble and a squawk and with astonishing celerity he would wring her neck and strip off her feathers. Another pet coon was allowed to range over the house at will, and finally had to be sent away because he had learned to open every door in the house, including cupboard doors, and could also open boxes and drawers left unlocked; and I have always believed he could have learned

A raccoon and a skunk share cat food in a suburban yard

to unlock drawers if he had been given the key. All coons are very curious, and one way of trapping them is to suspend above the trap a bit of bright tin; in solving this glittering mystery, traps are forgotten.

LESSON

Leading thought— The raccoon lives in hollow trees or caves along the banks of streams. It sleeps during the day and seeks its food at night. It sleeps during the winter.

Method— If there are raccoons in the vicinity, ask the older boys to look for their tracks near the streams and to describe them very carefully to the class. The ideal method of studying the animal, is to have a pet coon where the children may watch at leisure its entertaining and funny performances. If this is impossible, then follow the less desirable method of having the pupils read about the habits of the coon and thus arouse their interest and open their eyes, so that they may make observations of their own when opportunity offers. I would suggest the following topics for oral or written work in English:

"How and Where Coons Live and What They Do;" "The Autobiography of a Coon One Year Old;" "The Queer Antics of Pet Coons;" "Stories of the Coon's Relative, the Bear."

Observations—

1. Where have you found raccoon tracks? How do they differ from those of fox or dog? How far are the footprints apart? Can you see the heel and toe prints? Do you see the tracks of all four feet? Are the tracks in a straight line like those of the cat? What is the size of the track, the length, the breadth?

2. What do coons eat and how do they get their food? Which of

our crops are they likely to damage? What other damage do they do? Have you ever heard coons cry or whistle during August nights in the cornfields?

3. Why do raccoons like to live near the water? What do they find of interest there? How do they prepare their meat before eating it? How does a coon handle its meat while eating it?

4. What kind of fur has the coon? Why does it need such a heavy covering? Describe the color of the fur. Describe the tail. Of what use is such a large and bushy tail to this animal?

5. Describe the coon's face. How is it marked? What is its expression? Describe the eyes and ears. The nose. Has it teeth resembling those of the cat and dog?

6. Describe the coon's feet. How many toes on the front feet? How many on the hind feet? How does this differ from the cat and dog? How do the front and hind feet differ in appearance? Can both be used as hands?

7. How do coons arrange themselves for a nap in a tree? How do they cover the head? How is the tail used? Do you think this bushy tail used in this way would help to keep the animal warm in winter? Do coons sleep most daytimes or nights?

8. At what time of year are coons fattest? Leanest? Why? Do they ever come out of their nests in winter? Do they live together or singly in winter?

9. At what time of year are the young coons born? Do you know how they look when they are young? How are they cared for by their parents?

10. Are the coon's movements slow or fast? What large animal is a near relative of the coon?

Supplementary reading—American Animals, Stone and Cram; Wild Neighbors, Ingersoll; Familiar Life of Field and Forest, Mathews; Little People of the Sycamore, Roberts; Life of Animals, Ingersoll; "Mux" in Roof and Meadow, Sharp; Little Brother of the Bear, Long.

The Wolf

THE study of the wolf should precede the lessons on the fox and the dog. After becoming familiar with the habits of wolves, the pupils will be much better able to understand the nature of the dog and its life as a wild animal. In most localities, the study of the wolf must, of course, be a matter of reading, unless the pupils have an opportunity to study the animal in traveling menageries or in zoological gardens. However, in all the government preserves, the timber wolf has multiplied to such an extent, that it may become a factor in the lives of many people in the United States. This wolf ranged in packs over New York State a hundred years ago, but was finally practically exterminated in most of the eastern forests, except in remote and mountainous localities. A glance at Bulletin 72 by Vernon Bailey, published by the U. S. Department of Agriculture, Forest Service, is a revelation of the success of the timber wolf, in coming back to his own, as soon as the forest preserves furnished plenty of game, and forbade hunters. Timber wolves are returning of late years to Western Maine and Northern New Hampshire; Northern Michigan and Wisconsin have them in greater numbers; some have also

Wolves, seldom seen now, once ranged over many parts of North America

Eastern wolf

been killed in the Appalachian Mountains of Tennessee, Virginia and West Virginia, but their stronghold is in the great Rocky Mountain Region and the Northwestern Sierras, from which they have never been driven.

It might be well to begin this lesson on the wolf with a talk about the gray wolves which our ancestors had to contend with, and also with stories of the coyote or prairie wolf which has learned to adapt itself to civilization and flourishes in the regions west of the Rocky Mountains, despite men and dogs. Literature is rich in wolf stories. Although Kipling's famous Mowgli Stories belong to the realm of fiction, yet they contain interesting accounts of the habits of the wolves of India, and are based upon the hunter's and tracker's knowledge of these animals. We have many thrillingly interesting stories in our own literature which deal with our native wolves. The following are among the best:

"Lobo" in *Wild Animals I Have Known*; "Tito" in *Lives of the Hunted*; "Bad Lands Billy and the Winnipeg Wolf" in *Animal Heroes*, all by Thompson Seton; "The Passing of Black Whelps" in *Watchers of the Trail* by Roberts; *Northern Trails* by Long; "Pico, Coyote" by Coolidge in *True Tales of Birds and Beasts*.

For more serious accounts of the wolves see *American Animals*, p. 277; The "Hound of the Plains" in *Wild Neighbors*, and page 188 in *The Life of Animals*, both by Ingersoll. "The Coyote" by Bret Harte and "The Law of the Pack" in *The Second Jungle Book* bring the wolf into poetry.

From some or all of these stories, the pupils should get information about the habits of the wolves. This information should be incorporated in an essay or an oral exercise and should cover the following points: Where do the wolves live? On what do they feed? How do they get their prey? Do they hunt alone or in packs? How do they call to each other? Description of the den where the young are reared. The wolf's cleverness in eluding hunters and traps.

The Fox

TEACHER'S STORY

D O WE not always, on a clear morning of winter, feel a thrill that must have something primitive in its quality, at seeing certain tracks in the snow that somehow suggest wildness and freedom! Such is the track of the fox. Although it is somewhat like that of a small dog yet it is very different. The fox has longer legs than most dogs of his weight, and there is more of freedom in his track and more of strength and agility expressed in it. His gait is usually an easy lope; this places the imprint of three feet in a line, one ahead of another, but the fourth is off a little at one side, as if to keep the balance.

The fox lives in a den or burrow. The only fox home which I ever saw, was a rather deep cave beneath the roots of a stump, and there was no burrow or retreat beyond it. However, foxes often select woodchuck burrows, or make burrows of their own, and if they are caught within, they can dig rapidly, as many a hunter can attest. The mother usually selects an open place for a den for the young foxes; often an open field or side-hill is chosen for this. The den is carpeted with grass and is a very comfortable place for the fox puppies. The den of the father fox is usually not far away.

The face of the red fox shows plainly why he has been able to cope with man, and thrive despite and because of him. If ever a face showed cunning, it is his. Its pointed, slender nose gives it an expression of extreme cleverness, while the width of the head between the upstanding, triangular ears gives room for a brain of power. In color the fox is russet-red, the hind quarters being grayish. The legs are black outside and white inside; the throat is white, and the broad, triangular ears are tipped with black. The glory of the fox is his "brush," as the beautiful, bushy tail is called. This is red, with black toward the end and white-tipped. This tail is not merely for beauty, for it affords the fox warmth during the winter, as any one may see who has observed the way it is wrapped around the sleeping animal. But this bushy tail is a disadvantage, if it becomes bedraggled and heavy with snow and sleet, when the hounds are giving close chase to its owner. The silver fox and the black fox are the same species as the red fox.

The fox is an inveterate hunter of the animals of the field; meadow mice, rabbits, woodchucks, frogs, snakes and grasshoppers, are all acceptable food; he is also destructive of birds. His fondness for the latter has given him a bad reputation with the farmer because of his attacks on poultry. Not only will he raid hen-roosts if he can force entrance, but he catches many fowls in the summer when they are wandering through the fields. The way he carries the heavy burden of his larger prey shows his cleverness: He slings a hen or a goose over his shoulders, keeping the head in his mouth to steady the burden. Mr. Cram says, in American Animals:

"Yet, although the farmer and the fox are such inveterate enemies, they manage to benefit each other in a great many ways quite unintentionally. The fox destroys numberless field mice and woodchucks for the farmer and in return the farmer supplies him with poultry, and builds convenient bridges over streams and wet places, which the fox crosses oftener than the farmer, for he is as sensitive as a cat about getting his feet wet. On the whole, I am inclined to believe that the fox gets the best part of the exchange, for, while the farmer shoots at him on every occasion, and hunts him with dogs in the winter, he has cleared the land of wolves and panthers, so that foxes are probably safer than before any land was ploughed."

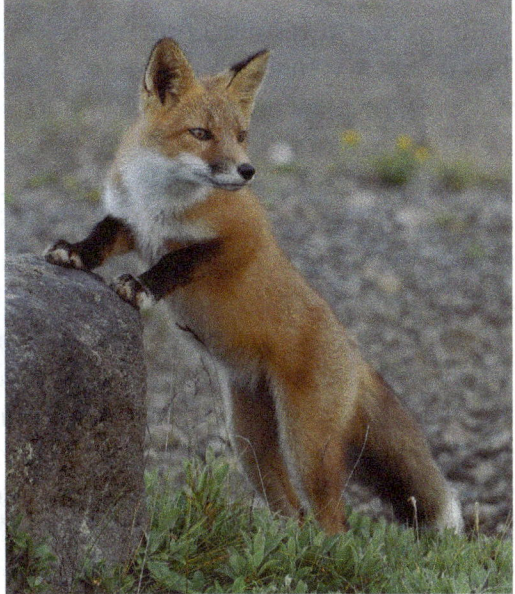

The bark of the fox is a high, sharp yelp, more like the bark of the coyote than of the dog. There is no doubt a considerable range of meaning in the fox's language, of which we are ignorant. He growls when angry, and when pleased he smiles like a dog and wags his beautiful tail.

Many are the wiles of the fox to head off dogs following his track: he often retraces his own steps for a few yards and then makes a long sidewise jump; the dogs go on, up to the end of the trail pocket, and try in vain to get the scent from that point. Sometimes he walks along the top rails of fences or takes the high and dry ridges where the scent will not remain; he often follows roads and beaten paths and also goes around and around in the midst of a herd of cattle, so that his scent is hidden; he crosses streams on logs and invents various other devices too numerous and intricate to describe. When chased by dogs, he naturally runs in a circle, probably so as not to be too far from home. If there are young ones in the den, the father fox leads the hounds far away, in the next county, if possible. Perhaps one of the most clever tricks of the fox, is to make friends with the dogs. I have known of two instances where a dog and fox were daily companions and playfellows.

The young foxes are born in the spring. They are black at first and are fascinating little creatures, being exceedingly playful and active. Their parents are very devoted to them, and during all their puppyhood, the mother fox is a menace to the poultry of the region, because the necessity is upon her of feeding her rapidly growing litter.

In my opinion, the best story of animal fiction is "Red Fox" by Roberts. Like all good fiction, it is based upon facts and it presents a wholesome picture of the life of the successful fox. "The Silver Fox" by Thompson Seton is another interesting and delightful story. Although the Nights with Uncle Remus could scarcely be called nature stories, yet they are interesting in showing how the fox has become a part of folk-lore.

LESSON

Leading thought—The red fox is so clever that it has been able, in many parts of our country, to maintain itself despite dogs and men.

Method— This lesson is likely to be given largely from hearsay or reading. However, if the school is in a rural district, there will be plenty of hunters' stories afloat, from which may be elicited facts concerning the cunning and cleverness of the red fox. In such places there is also the opportunity in winter to study fox tracks upon the snow. The lesson may well be given when there are fox tracks for observation. The close relationship between foxes and dogs should be emphasized.

Observations and reading—

1. Describe the fox's track. How does it differ from the track of a small dog?

2. Where does the fox make its home? Describe the den. Describe the den in which the young foxes live.

3. Describe the red fox, its color and form as completely as you can. What is the expression of its face? What is there peculiar about its tail? What is the use of this great bushy tail in the winter?

Red fox cubs

4. What is the food of the fox? How does it get its food? Is it a day or a night hunter? How does the fox benefit the farmer? How does it injure him? How does the fox carry home its heavy game, such as a goose or a hen?

5. Have you ever heard the fox bark? Did it sound like the bark of a dog? How does the fox express anger? Pleasure?

6. When chased by dogs, in what direction does the fox run? Describe all of the tricks which you know by which the fox throws the dog off the scent.

7. When are the young foxes born? How many in a litter? What color are they? How do they play with each other? How do they learn to hunt?

Supplementary reading— *Red Fox* by Roberts; *Silver Fox* by Thompson Seton; *Little Beasts of Field and Wood*, page 25; *Squirrels and Other Fur Bearers*, chapter 7; Fox Ways in *Ways of Wood Folk*; The Springfield Fox in *Wild Animals I Have Known*; *Familiar Wild Animals*; *Familiar Life in Field and Forest*, page 213; *American Animals*, page 264; *Nights with Uncle Remus*.

A Belgian sheperd and a border collie playing

Dogs

NOT only to-day but in ancient days, before the dawn of history, the dog was the companion of man. Whether the wild species from whence he sprang, was wolf or jackal or some other similar animal, we do not know, but we do know that many types of dogs have been tamed independently by savages, in the region where their untamed relatives run wild. As the whelps of wolves, jackals and foxes are all easily tamed, and are most interesting little creatures, we can understand how they became companions to the children of the savage and barbarous peoples who hunted them.

In the earliest records of cave dwellers, in the picture writing of the ancient Egyptians and of other ancient peoples, we find record of the presence and value of the dog. But man, in historical times, has been able to evolve breeds that vary more in form than do the wild species of the present. There are 200 distinct breeds of dogs known to-day, and many of these have been bred for special purposes. The paleontologists, moreover, assure us that there has been a decided advance in the size and quality of the dog's brain since the days of his savagery; thus, he has been the companion of man's civilization also. It is not, therefore, to be wondered at that the dog is now the most companionable, and has the most human qualities and intelligence of all our domesticated animals.

Dogs run down their prey; it is a necessity, therefore, that they be equipped with legs that are long, strong and muscular. The cat, which jumps for her prey, has much more delicate legs but has powerful hips to enable her to leap. The dog's feet are much more heavily padded than those of the cat, because in running, he must not stop to save his feet. Hounds often return from a chase with bleeding feet, despite the heavy pads, but the wounds are usually cuts between the toes. The claws are heavy and are not retractile; thus, they afford a protection to the feet when running, and they are also used for digging out game which burrows into the ground. They are not used for grasping prey like those of the cat and are used only incidentally in fighting, while the cat's claws are the most

SVENSKA MÄSSAN (CC BY 2.0)
Boston terrier. This small popular breed is one of the few to originate in America. It is very companionable and highly intelligent

CLAUDE VALROFF (CC BY-SA 2.0)
Beagle. These hounds hunt individually, in pairs, or in packs; they are chiefly used for hunting rabbits

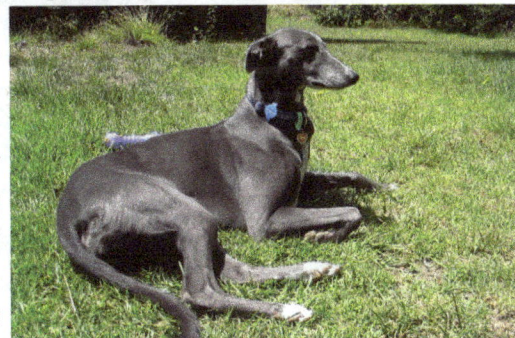

SHAZ91 (CC BY 3.0)
Greyhound. This swiftest of all large dogs hunts by sight

St. Bernard. These dogs stand about thirty inches high and have an average weight of 175 pounds

Pointer. These dogs are called pointers because of their habit of pointing at the concealed game birds they have scented.

Beagle pup. Beagles are small models of foxhounds; they are not so swift as foxhounds, but seem to have a keener sense of smell

important weapons in her armory. It is an interesting fact that Newfoundland dogs, which are such famous swimmers, have their toes somewhat webbed.

The dog's body is long, lean, and very muscular, a fat dog being usually pampered and old. The coat is of hair and is not of fine fur like that of the cat. It is of interest to note that the Newfoundland dog has an inner coat of fine hair comparable to that of the mink or muskrat. When a dog is running, his body is extended to its fullest length; in fact, it seems to "lie flat," the outstretched legs heightening the effect of extreme muscular effort of forward movement. A dog is master of several gaits; he can run, walk, trot, bound and crawl.

The iris of the

dog's eye is usually of a beautiful brown, although this varies with breeds; in puppies, the iris is usually blue. The pupil is round like our own; and dogs cannot see well in the dark like the cat, but in daylight they have keen sight. The nose is so much more efficient than the eyes, that it is on the sense of smell the dog depends for following his prey and for recognizing friend and foe. The damp, soft skin that covers the nose, has in its dampness the conditions for carrying the scent to the wide nostrils; these are situated at the most forward part of the face, and thus may be lifted in any direction to receive the marvelous impressions, so completely beyond our comprehension. Think of being able to scent the track of a fox made several hours previously. Not only to scent it, but to follow by scent for many miles without ever having a glimpse of the fleeing foe! In fact, while running, the dog's attention seems to be focused entirely upon the sense of smell, for I have seen hounds pass within a few rods to the windward of the fox they were chasing, without observing him at all. When the nose of any of the moist-nosed beasts, such as cattle and dogs, becomes dry it is a sign of illness.

A light fall of damp snow gives the dog the best conditions for following a track by scent and a hound, when on the trail, will run until exhausted. There are many authentic observations which show that hounds have followed a fox for twenty-four hours without food, and probably with little rest.

The dog's weapons for battle, like those of the wolf, are his tushes: with these, he holds and tears his prey; with them, he seizes the woodchuck or other small animal through the back and shakes its life out. In fighting a larger animal, the dog leaps against it and often incidentally tears its flesh with his strong claws; but he does not strike a blow with his foot like the cat, nor can he hold his quarry with it.

Dog's teeth are especially fitted for their work. The incisors are small and sharp; the canine teeth or tushes are very long, but there are bare spaces on the jaws so that they are able to cross past each other; the molar teeth are not fitted for grinding, like the teeth of a cow, but are especially fitted for cutting, as may be noted if we watch the way a dog gnaws bones, first gnawing with the back teeth on one side and then on the other. In fact, a dog does not seem to need to chew

English springer spaniel. No other family of dogs contains so many recognized breeds as the spaniel family--seven hunting and two toy breeds. Formerly these dogs were trained to flush or "spring" the game so that swifter dogs or falcons could catch it; today they are popular as all-purpose dogs

A bearded collie. Collies show great intelligence in the herding of various kinds of domestic animals; they have long been used in Scotland, but their popularity has spread to may other countries. The one pictured here is a show dog

anything, but simply needs to cut his meat in small enough pieces so that he can gulp them down without chewing. His powers of digesting unchewed food are something that the hustling American may well envy.

Of all domestic animals, the dog is most humanly understandable in expressing emotions. If delighted, he leaps about giving ecstatic little barks and squeals, his tail in the air and his eyes full of happy anticipation. If he wishes to be friendly, he looks at us interestedly, comes over to smell of us in order to assure himself whether he has ever met us before, and then wags his tail as a sign of good faith. If he wishes to show affection, he leaps upon us and licks our face or hands with his soft, deft tongue and follows us jealously. When he stands at attention, he holds his tail stiff in the air, and looks up with one ear lifted as if to say, "Well, what's doing?" When angry, he growls and shows his teeth and the tail is held rigidly out behind, as if to convince us that it is really a continuation of his backbone. When afraid, he whines and lies flat upon his belly, often looking beseechingly up toward his master as if begging not to be punished; or he crawls away out of sight. When ashamed, he drops his tail between his legs and with drooping head and sidewise glance slinks away. When excited, he barks and every bark expresses high nervous tension.

Almost all dogs that chase their prey, bark when so doing, which would seem at first sight to be a foolish thing to do, in that it reveals their whereabouts to their victims and also adds an incentive to flight. But it must be borne in mind that dogs are descended from wolves, which naturally hunt in packs and do not stalk their prey. The baying of the hound is a most common example of the habit, and as we listen we can understand how, by following this sound, the pack is kept

ANTONIO CRUZ (CC BY 3.0)

A Seeing Eye dog. The training of dogs to lead the blind began in the United States; the same methods have now become popular in Europe. The Seeing Eye has headquarters in New York City

ELF (CC BY-SA 3.0)

An english setter. This breed originated in England from a cross between a field spaniel and a pointer

St. Bernard. This breed of huge dogs was developed by monks in the Swiss Alps to aid in the rescue of people lost in the mountains

together. Almost all breeds of dogs have an acute sense of hearing. When a dog bays at the moon or howls when he hears music, it is simply a reversion to the wild habit of howling to call together the pack or in answer "to the music of the pack." It is interesting that our music, which is the flower of our civilization, should awaken the sleeping ancestral traits in the canine breast. But perhaps that, too, is why we respond to music, because it awakens in us the strong, primitive emotions, and, for the time, enables us to free ourselves from all conventional shackles and trammels.

LESSON

Leading thought— The dog is a domesticated descendant of wolf-like animals and has retained certain of the habits and characteristics of his ancestors.

Method— For the observation lesson it would be well to have at hand, a well-disposed dog which would not object to being handled; a collie or a hound would be preferable. Many of the questions should be given to the pupils to answer from observations at home, and the lesson should be built upon the experience of the pupils with dogs.

Observations—

1. Why are the legs of the dog long and strong in proportion to the body compared with those of the cat?

2. Compare the feet of the cat with those of the dog and note which has the heavier pads. Why is this of use to each?

3. Which has the stronger and heavier claws, the dog or the cat? Can the dog retract his claws so that they are not visible, as does the

cat? Of what use is this arrangement to the dog? Are the front feet just like the hind feet? How many toe impressions show in the track of the dog?

4. What is the general characteristic of the body of the dog? Is it soft like that of the cat, or lean and muscular? What is the difference between the hair covering of the dog and cat? What is the attitude of the dog when running fast? How many kinds of gaits has he?

5. In general, how do the eyes of the dog differ from those of the cat? Does he rely as much upon his eyes for finding his prey as does the cat? Can a dog see in the dark? What is the color of the dog's eyes?

6. Study the ear of the dog; is it covered? Is this outer ear movable, is it a flap, or is it cornucopia shaped? How is this flap used when the dog is listening? Roll a sheet of paper into a flaring tube and place the small end upon your own ear, and note if it helps you to hear better the sounds in the direction toward which the tube opens. Note how the hound lifts his long earlaps, so as to make a tube for conveying sounds to his inner ear. Do you think that dogs can hear well?

7. What is the position of the nose in the dog's face? Of what use is this? Describe the nostrils; are they placed on the foremost point of the face? What is the condition of the skin that surrounds them? How does this condition of the nose aid the dog? What other animals have it? Does the dog recognize his friends or become acquainted with strangers by means of his sight or of his powers of smelling?

8. How long after a fox or rabbit has passed can a hound follow the track? Does he follow it by sight or by smell? What are the conditions most favorable for retaining the scent? The most unfavorable? How long will a hound follow a fox trail without stopping for rest or food? Do you think the dog is your superior in ability to smell?

9. How does a dog seize and kill his prey? How does he use his feet and claws when fighting? What are his especially strong weapons? Describe a dog's teeth and explain the reason for the bare spaces on the jaw next to the tushes. Does the dog use his tushes when chewing? What teeth does he use when gnawing a bone? Make a diagram of the arrangement of the dog's teeth.

10. How by action, voice, and especially by the movement of the tail does the dog express the following emotions: Delight, friendliness, af-

fection, attention, anger, fear, shame, excitement? How does he act when chasing his prey? Why do wolves and dogs bark when following the trail? Do you think of a reason why dogs often howl at night or when listening to music? What should we feed to our pet dogs? What should we do to make them comfortable in other ways?

11. Tell or write a story of some dog of which you know by experience or hearsay. Of what use was the dog to the pioneer? How are dogs used in the Arctic regions? In Holland?

12. How many breeds of dogs do you know? Describe characters of such as follows: The length of the legs as compared with the body; the general shape of the body, head, ears, nose; color and character of hair on head, body and tail.

13. Find if you can the reasons which have led to the developing of the following breeds: Newfoundland, St. Bernard, mastiffs, hounds, collies, spaniels, setters, pointers, bulldogs, terriers, and pugs.

Supplementary reading— "Stories of Brave Dogs" from *St. Nicholas,* the Century Co.; the following three stories from Thompson-Seton: "Chink" in *Lives of the Hunted*, "Snap" in *Animal Heroes*, "Wully" in *Wild Animals I Have Known*; *Bob, Son of Battle*; *Mack, His Book*, by Florence Leigh; *Rab and his Friends*; *The Dog of Flanders*; "Red Dog" in Kipling's Jungle Stories; *Animals of the World*, Knight and Jenks, p. 80; *Life of Animals*, Ingersoll, p. 187.

Baby cats are called kittens

The Cat

TEACHER'S STORY

F all people, the writer should regard the cat sympathetically, for when she was a baby of five months she was adopted by a cat. My self-elected foster-mother was Jenny, a handsome black and white cat, which at that time lost her first litter of kittens, through the attack of a savage cat from the woods. She was as Rachel crying for her children, when she seemed suddenly to comprehend that I, although larger than she, was an infant. She haunted my cradle, trying to give me milk from her own breasts; and later she brought half-killed mice and placed them enticingly in my cradle, coaxing me to play with them, a performance which pleased me much more than it did my real mother. Jenny always came to comfort me when I cried, rubbing against me, purring loudly, and licking me with her tongue in a way to drive mad the modern mother, wise as to the sources of children's internal parasites. This maternal attitude toward me lasted as long as Jenny lived, which was until I was nine years old. Never during those years did I lift my voice

in wailing, that she did not come to comfort me; and even to-day I can remember how great that comfort was, especially when my naughtiness was the cause of my weeping, and when, therefore, I felt that the whole world, except Jenny, was against me.

Jenny was a cat of remarkable intelligence and was very obedient and useful. Coming down the kitchen stairs one day, she played with the latch and someone hearing her, opened the door. She did this several times, when one day she chanced to push down the latch, and thus opened the door herself. After that, she always opened it herself. A little later, she tried the trick on other doors, and soon succeeded in opening all the latched doors in the house, by thrusting one front leg through the handle, and thus supporting her weight, and pressing down with the foot of the other on the thumb-piece of the latch. I remember, guests were greatly astonished to see her coming thus swinging into the sitting-room. Later she tried the latches from the other side, jumping up and trying to lift the hook; but now, her weight was thrown against the wrong side of the door for opening, and she soon ceased this futile waste of energy; but for several years, she let herself into all the rooms in this clever manner, and taught a few of her bright kittens to do the same.

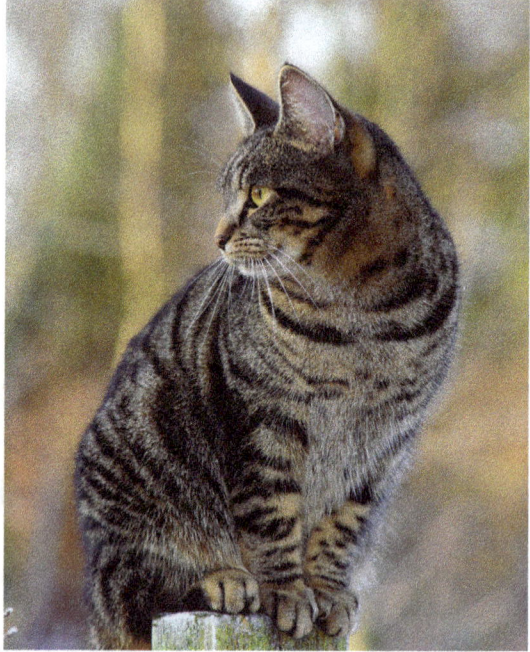

A pet cat enjoys long conversations with favored members of the household. She will sit in front of her mistress and mew, with every appearance of answering the questions addressed her; and since the cat and the mistress each knows her own part of the conversation, it is perhaps more typical of society chatter than we might like to confess. Of our language, the cat learns to understand the call to food, its own name, "scat," and "No, No," probably inferring the meaning of the latter from the tone of voice. On the other hand, we understand when it asks to go out, and its polite recognition to the one who opens the door. I knew one cat which invariably thanked us when we let him in as well as out. When the cat is hungry, it mews pleadingly;

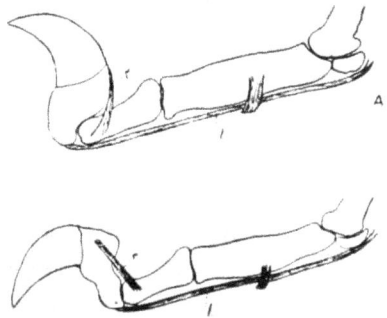

Bones and Ligaments of Cat's Claw.
A. Claw up. B. Claw thrust out.

when happy in front of the fire, it looks at us sleepily out of half-closed eyes and gives a short mew expressive of affection and content; or it purrs, a noise which we do not know how to imitate and which expresses perfectly the happiness of intimate companionship. When frightened the cat yowls, and when hurt squalls shrilly; when fighting, it is like a savage warrior in that it howls a war-song in blood-curdling strains, punctuated with a spitting expressive of fear and contempt; and unfortunately, its love song is scarcely less agonizing to the listener. The cat's whole body enters into the expression of its emotions. When feeling affectionate toward its mistress, it rubs against her gown, with tail erect, and vibrating with a purr which seems fundamental. When angry, it lays its ears back and lashes its tail back and forth, the latter being a sign of excitement; when frightened, its hair stands on end, especially the hair of the tail, making that expressive appendage twice its natural size; when caught in disobedience, the cat lets its tail droop, and when running lifts it in a curve.

While we feed cats milk and scraps from our own table, they have never become entirely civilized in their tastes. They always catch mice and other small animals and prove pestiferous in destroying birds. Jenny was wont to bring her quarry, as an offering, to the front steps of our home every night; one morning we found seven mice, a cotton-tail rabbit and two snakes, which represented her night's catch. The cat never chases its prey like the dog. It discovers the haunts of its victims, and then lies in ambush, flattened out as still as a statue and all its feet beneath it, ready to make the spring. The weight of the body is a factor which enters in the blow with which the cat strikes down its victim, and thus stuns and which it later kills by gripping the throat with the strong tushes. She carries her victims as she does her kittens, by the back.

The cat's legs are not long compared with the body, and it runs with a leaping gallop; the upper legs are armed with powerful muscles. It walks on the padded toes, five on the front feet and four on the hind feet. The cat needs its claws to be sharp and hooked, in order to seize and hold its prey, so they are kept safely sheathed when not thus used. If the claws struck the earth during walking, as do the dog's, they would soon become dulled. When sharpening its claws it reaches high up against a tree or post, and strikes them into the wood with a downward scratch; this act is probably more for exercising the muscles which control the claws than for sharpening them.

The cat's track is in a single line as if it had only two feet, one set directly ahead of the other. It accomplishes this by setting its hind feet exactly in the tracks made by the front feet. The cat can easily leap upward, landing on a window-sill five feet from the ground. The jump is made with the hind legs and the alighting is done silently on the front feet.

Cats' eyes are fitted for seeing in the dark; in the daytime the pupil is simply a narrow, up and down slit; under excitement, and at night, the pupil covers almost the entire eye. At the back of the eye is a reflecting surface, which catches such dim light as there is, and by reflecting it enables the cat to use it twice. It is this reflected light, which gives the peculiar green glare to the eyes of all the cats when seen in the dark. Some night-fly-

In the daytime the pupil is just a slit

ing moths have a like arrangement for utilizing the light, and their eyes glow like living coals. Of course, since the cat is a night hunter, this power of multiplying the rays of light is of great use. The

Notice the sharp teeth and raspy tongue

iris of the eye is usually yellow, but in kittens it may be blue or green.

The cat's teeth are peculiarly fitted for its needs. The six doll-like incisors of the upper and lower jaw are merely for scraping meat from bones. The two great tushes, or canines, on each jaw, with a bare place behind so that they pass each other freely, are sharp and hooked, and are for seizing and carrying prey. The cat is able to open its mouth as wide as a right angle, in order to better hold and carry prey. The back teeth, or molars, are four on each side in the upper jaw and three, below. They are sharp-edged wedges made for cutting meat fine enough, so that it may be swallowed.

The tongue is covered with sharp papillae directed backwards, also used for rasping juices from meat. The cat's nose is moist, and her sense of smell very keen, as is also her sense of hearing. The ears rise like two hollow half-cones on either side of the head and are filled with sensitive hairs; they ordinarily open forward, but are capable of movement. The cat's whiskers consist of from twenty-five to thirty long hairs set in four lines, above and at the sides of the mouth; they are connected with sensitive nerves and are therefore true feelers. The cat's fur is very fine and thick, and is also sensitive; as can readily be proved, by trying to stroke it the wrong way. While the wild cats have gray or tawny fur, variously mottled or shaded, the more striking colors we see in the domestic cats are the result of man's breeding.

Cats are very cleanly in their habits. Puss always washes her face directly after eating, using one paw for a wash-cloth and licking it clean after she rubs her face. She cleans her fur with her rough tongue and also by biting; and she promptly buries objectionable matter. The mother cat is very attentive to the cleanliness of her kittens, licking them clean from nose tip to tail tip. The ways of the mother cat with her kittens do much to sustain the assertions of Mr. Seton and Mr. Long that young animals are trained and educated by their parents. The cat brings half-dazed mice to her kittens, that they may learn to follow and catch them with their own little claws. When she punishes them, she cuffs the ears by holding one side of the kitten's head firm with the claws of one foot, while she lays on the blows with the other. She carries her kittens by the nape of the neck, never hurting them. She takes them into the field when they are old enough, and shows them the haunts of mice, and does many things for their education and welfare. The kittens meantime train themselves to agility and dexterity, by playing rough and tumble with each other, and by chasing every small moving object, even to their own tails.

The cat loves warmth and finds her place beneath the stove or at the hearthside. She likes some people, and dislikes others, for no reason we can detect. She can be educated to be friendly with dogs and with birds. In feeding her, we should give her plenty of sweet milk, some cooked meat and fish of which she is very fond; and we should keep a bundle of catnip to make her happy, for even the larger cats of the wilderness seem to have a passionate liking for this herb. The cat laps milk with her rough tongue, and when eating meat, she turns the head this way and that, to cut the tough muscle with her back teeth.

CATS SHOULD BE TRAINED TO LEAVE BIRDS ALONE

Every owner of a cat owes it to the world to train puss to leave birds alone. If this training is begun during kittenhood, by switching the culprit every time it even looks at a bird, it will soon learn to leave them severely alone. I have tried this many times, and I know it is efficacious, if the cat is intelligent. We have never had a cat whose early training we controlled, that could ever be induced to even watch birds. If a cat is not thus trained as a kitten, it is likely to be always treacher-

Cats will kill many small animals, including birds if not trained otherwise

ous in this respect. But in case any one has a valuable cat which is given to catching birds, I strongly advise the following treatment which has been proved practicable by a friend of mine. When a cat has made the catch, take the bird away and sprinkle it with red pepper, and then give it back. One such treatment as this resulted in making one cat, which was an inveterate bird hunter, run and hide every time he saw a bird thereafter. Any persons taking cats with them to their summer homes, and abandoning them there to prey upon the birds of the vicinity, and to become poor, half-starved, wild creatures, ought to be arrested and fined. It is not only cruelty to the cats, but it is positive injury and damage to the community, because of the slaughter of beneficial birds which it entails.

LESSON

Leading thought— The cat was made a domestic animal before man wrote histories. It gets prey by springing from ambush and is fitted by form of body and teeth to do this. It naturally hunts at night and has eyes fitted to see in the dark.

Method— This lesson may be used in primary grades by asking a

few questions at a time and allowing the children to make their observations on their own kittens at home, or a kitten may be brought to school for this purpose. The upper grade work consists of reading and retelling or writing exciting stories of the great, wild, savage cats, like the tiger, lion, leopard, lynx and panther.

Observations—

1. How much of Pussy's language do you understand? What does she say when she wishes you to open the door for her? How does she ask for something to eat? What does she say when she feels like conversing with you? How does she cry when hurt? When frightened? What noise does she make when fighting? When calling other cats? What are her feelings when she purrs? When she spits? How many things which you say does she understand?

2. How else than by voice does she express affection, pleasure and anger? When she carries her tail straight up in the air is she in a pleasant mood? When her tail "bristles up" how does she feel? What is it a sign of, when she lashes her tail back and forth?

3. What do you feed to cats? What do they catch for themselves?

What do the cats that are wild live upon? How does the cat help us? How does she injure us?

4. How does a cat catch her prey? Does she track mice by the scent? Does she catch them by running after them as a dog does? Describe how she lies in ambush. How does she hold the mouse as she pounces upon it? How does she carry it home to her kittens?

5. Study the cat's paws to see how she holds her prey. Where are the sharp claws? Are they always in sight like a dog's? Does she touch them to the ground when she walks? Which walks the more silently, a dog or a cat? Why? Describe the cat's foot, including the toe-pads. Are there as many toes on the hind feet as on the front feet? What kind of a track does the cat make in the snow? How does she set her feet to make such a track? How does she sharpen her claws? How does she use her claws for climbing? How far have you ever seen a cat jump? Does she use her front or her hind feet in making the jump? On which feet does she alight? Does she make much noise when she alights?

6. What is there peculiar about a cat's eyes? What is their color? What is the color of kittens' eyes? What is the shape of the pupil in daylight? In the dark? Describe the inner lid which comes from the corner of the eye.

7. How many teeth has Puss? What is the use of the long tushes? Why is there a bare space behind these? What does she use her little front teeth for? Does she use her back teeth for chewing or for cutting meat?

8. How many whiskers has she? How long are they? What is their use? Do you think that puss has a keen sense of smell? Why do you think so? Do you think she has a keen sense of hearing? How do the shape and position of the ears help in listening? In what position are the ears when puss is angry?

9. How many colors do you find in our domestic cats. What is the color of wild cats? Why would it not be beneficial to the wild-cat to have as striking colors as our tame cats? Compare the fur of the cat with the hair of the dog. How do they differ? If a cat chased her prey like the dog do you think her fur would be a too warm covering?

10. Describe how the cat washes her face. How does she clean her fur? How does her rough tongue help in this? How does the mother cat wash her kittens?

11. How does a little kitten look when a day or two old? How long

Young cats love playing

before its eyes open? How does the cat carry her kittens? How does a kitten act when it is being carried? How does the mother cat punish her kittens? How does she teach them to catch mice? How do kittens play? How does the exercise they get in playing fit them to become hunters?

12. How should cats be trained not to touch birds? When must this training begin? Why should a person be punished for injury to the public who takes cats to summer cottages and leaves them there to run wild?

13. Where in the room does puss best like to lie? How does she sun herself? What herb does she like best? Does she like some people and not others? What strange companions have you known a cat to have? What is the cat's chief enemy? How should we care for and make the cat comfortable?

14. Write or tell stories on the following subjects: (1) The things which my pet cat does; (2) The Wild Cat; (3) The Lion; (4) The Tiger; (5) The Leopard; (6) The Panther and the Mountain Lion; (7) The Lynx; (8) The History of Domestic Cats; (9) The Different Races of Cats, describing the Manx, the Persian and the Angora Cats.

Supplementary reading— *The Life of Animals*, Ingersoll; *American Animals*, Stone and Cram; *Our Domestic Animals*, Burkett; *The Fireside Sphinx*, Repplier; *Concerning Cats*, Winslow; The following animal stories from *St. Nicholas* Magazine: Cat Stories, Lion and Tiger Stories, Panther Stories.

A young baby goat, or kid

The Goat

TEACHER'S STORY

LITTLE do we in America realize the close companionship that has existed in older countries, from time immemorial, between goats and people. This association began when man was a nomad, and took with him in his wanderings, his flocks, of which goats formed the larger part. He then drank their milk, ate their flesh, wove their hair into raiment, or made cloth of their pelts, and used their skins for water bags. Among peoples of the East all these uses continue to the present day. In the streets of Cairo, old Arabs may be seen with goat skins filled with water upon their backs; and in any city of Western Asia or Southern Europe, flocks of goats are driven along the streets to be milked in sight of the consumer.

In order to understand the goat's peculiarities of form and habit, we should consider it as a wild animal, living upon the mountain heights amid rocks and snow and scant vegetation. It is marvelously

CHRISTIANNAWROTH (CC BY-SA 4.0)
Saanen goat

sure-footed, and when on its native mountains, it can climb the sharpest crags and leap chasms. This peculiarity has been seized upon by showmen who often exhibit goats which walk on the tight rope with ease, and even turn themselves upon it without falling. The instinct for climbing still lingers in the domestic breeds, and in the country the goat may be seen on top of stone piles or other objects, while in city suburbs, its form may be discerned on the roofs of shanties and stables.

It is a common saying that a goat will eat anything, and much sport is made of this peculiarity. This fact has more meaning for us when we realize that wild goats live in high altitudes, where there is little plant life, and are, therefore, obliged to find sustenance on lichens, moss and such scant vegetation as they can find.

The goat is closely allied to the sheep, differing from it in only a few particulars; its horns rise from the forehead curving over backward and do not form a spiral like those of the ram; its covering is usually of hair, and the male has a beard from which we get the name goatee; the goat has no gland between the toes, and it does have a rank and disagreeable odor. In a wild state, it usually lives a little higher up the mountains than do the sheep, and it is a far more intelligent animal. Mary Austin says: "Goats lead naturally by reason of a quicker instinct, forage more freely and can find water on their own account, and give voice in case of alarm. Goat leaders exhibit jealousy of their rights to be first over the stepping-stones or to walk the teetering log bridges at the roaring creeks." On the great plains, it is a common usage to place a few goats in a flock of sheep, because of the greater sagacity of these animals as leaders, and also as defenders in case of attack.

Goats' teeth are arranged for cropping herbage and especially for browsing. There are six molar teeth on each side of each jaw; there are eight lower incisors and none above. The goat's sense of smell is very acute; the ears are movable and the sense of hearing is keen; the eyes are full and very intelligent; the horns are somewhat flattened and angular and often knobbed somewhat in front, and curve backward above the neck; they are, however, very efficient as weapons of defence. The legs are strong, though not large, and are well fitted for leaping and running. The feet have two hoofs, that is, the animal walks upon two toe-nails. There are two smaller toes behind and above the hoofs. The goat can run with great rapidity. The tail of the goat is short like that of the deer, and does not need to be amputated like that of the sheep. Although the normal covering of the goat is hair, there are some species which have a more or less woolly coat. When angry the goat shakes its head, and defends itself by butting with the head, also by striking with the horns, which are very sharp. Goats are very tractable and make affectionate pets when treated with kindness; they display far more affection for their owner than do sheep.

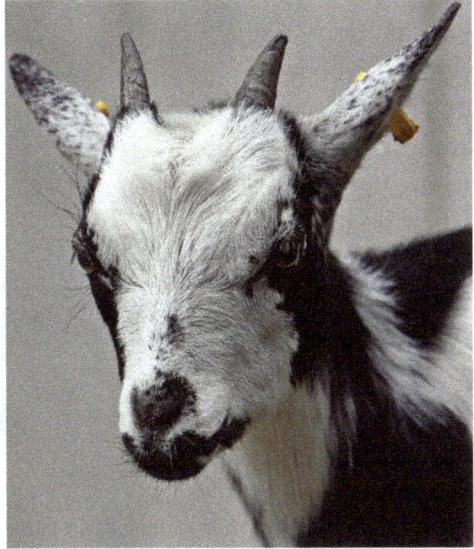

Our famous Rocky Mountain goat, although it belongs rather to the antelope family, is a large animal, and is the special prize of the hunter; however, it still holds its own in the high mountains of the Rocky and Cascade Ranges. Both sexes have slender black horns, white hair, and black feet, eyes and nose. Owen Wister says of this animal: "He is white, all white, and shaggy, and twice as large as any goat you ever saw. His white hair hangs long all over him like a Spitz dog's or an Angora cat's; and against its shaggy white mass the blackness of his hoofs and horns and nose looks particularly black. His legs are thick, his neck is thick, everything about him is thick, save only his thin black horns. They're generally about six (often more than nine) inches long, they spread very slightly, and they curve slightly backward. At their base they are a little rough, but as they rise they become cylindrically smooth and taper to an ugly point. His hoofs are heavy, broad and blunt. The female is lighter than the male, and with horns more slender, a trifle. And (to return to the question of diet) we visited the

A Toggenburg goat. This Swiss breed, developed by a careful selection of animals for many years, has attained a very definite standard of size, color, and conformation

pasture where the herd (of thirty-five) had been, and found no signs of grass growing or grass eaten; there was no grass on that mountain. The only edible substance was a moss, tufted, stiff and dry to the touch. I also learned that the goat is safe from predatory animals. With his impenetrable hide and his disemboweling horns he is left by the wolves and mountain lions respectfully alone." (See American Animals, p. 57; Camp Fires of a Naturalist, chapters VIII and XIII).

Milch Goats— Many breeds of these have been developed, and the highest type is, perhaps, found in Switzerland. The Swiss farmers have found the goat particularly adapted to their high mountains and have used it extensively; thus, goats developed in the Saane and Toggenburg valleys have a world-wide reputation. Above these valleys the high mountains are covered with perpetual snow, and winter sets in about November 1st, lasting until the last of May. The goats are kept with the cows in barns and fed upon hay; but as soon as the snow is gone from the valleys and the lower foot-hills, the cattle and goats are sent with the herders and boy assistants, to the grazing grounds. A bell is put upon the cow that leads the herd so as to keep it together and the boys, in their gay peasant dresses, are as happy as the playful calves and goats to get out in the spring sunshine. The herds follow the receding snows up the mountains until about midsummer, when

Angora goats

they reach the high places of scanty vegetation; then they start on the downward journey, returning to the home and stables about November 1st. The milk from goats is mixed with that from cows to make cheese, and this cheese has a wide reputation; some of the varieties are: Roquefort, Schweitzer and Altenburger. Although the cheese is excellent, the butter made from goat's milk is quite inferior to that made from the cow's. The milk, when the animals are well taken care of, is exceedingly nourishing; it is thought to be the best milk in the world for children. Usually, the trouble with goat's milk is, that the animals are not kept clean nor is care taken in milking. Germany has produced many distinct and excellent breeds of milch goats; the Island of Malta, Spain, England, Ireland, Egypt and Nubia have each developed noted breeds. Of all these, the Nubias give the most milk, sometimes yielding from four to six quarts per day, while an ordinary goat is considered fairly good if it yields two quarts per day.

The Mohair Goats— There are two noted breeds of goats whose hair is used extensively for weaving into fabrics; one of these is the Cashmere and the other the Angora. The Cashmere goat has long, straight, silky hair for an outside coat and has a winter under-coat of very delicate wool. There are not more than two or three ounces of this wool upon one goat, and this is made into the famous Cashmere shawls; ten goats furnish barely enough of this wool for one shawl. The Cashmere goats are grown most largely in Thibet, and the wool is shipped from the high tableland to the Valley of Cashmere, and is made into shawls. It requires the work of several people for a year to produce one

101

of these famous shawls.

The Angora goat has a long, silky and very curly fleece. These goats were first discovered in Angora, a city of Asia Minor south of the Black Sea, and some 200 miles southeast from Constantinople. The Angora goat is a beautiful and delicate animal, and furnishes most of the mohair, which is made into the cloths known as mohair, alpaca, camel's hair and many other fabrics. The Angora goat has been introduced into America, in California, Texas, Arizona, and to some extent in the Middle West. It promises to be a very profitable industry. (See Farmers' Bulletin No. 137, "The Angora Goat," United States Department of Agriculture.)

An American Alpine goat. These have been carefully cross-bred to create lots of fine milk in American conditions

The skins of goats are used extensively; morocco, gloves and many other articles are made from them. In the Orient, the skin of the goat is used as a bag in which to carry water and wine.

References— American Animals, p. 55; *Neighbors with Claws and Hoofs*, p. 190; *Familiar Animals*, pp. 169 and 183; *Camp Fires of a Naturalist*, chapters VIII and XIII; *Lives of Animals*.

LESSON

Leading thought— Goats are among our most interesting domesticated animals, and their history is closely interwoven with the history of the development of civilization. In Europe, their milk is made into

A herd of goats in Vallejo, California

cheese that has a world-wide fame; and from the hair of some of the species, beautiful fabrics are woven. The goat is naturally an animal of the high mountains.

Method— A span of goats harnessed to a cart is second only to ponies, in a child's estimation; therefore, the beginning of this lesson may well be a span of goats thus employed. The lesson should not be given unless the pupils have an opportunity for making direct observations on the animal's appearance and habits. There should be some oral and written work in English done with this lesson. Following are topics for such work: "The Milch Goat of Switzerland," "How Cashmere Shawls are Made," "The Angora Goat," "The Chamois."

Observations—

1. Do you think that goats like to climb to high points? Are they fitted to climb steep, inaccessible places? Can they jump off steep places in safety? How does it happen the goat is sure-footed? How do its legs and feet compare with those of the sheep?

2. What does the goat eat? Where does it find its natural food on mountains? How are the teeth arranged for cutting its food? Does a goat chew its cud like a cow?

3. What is the covering of the goat? Describe a billy-goat's beard.

Do you suppose this is for ornament? For what is goat's hair used?

4. Do you think the goat has a keen sense of sight, of hearing and of smell? Why? Why did it need to be alert and keen when it lived wild upon the mountains? Do you think the goat is intelligent? Give instances of this.

5. Describe the horns. Do they differ from the horns of the sheep? How does a goat fight? Does he strike head on, like the sheep, or sidewise? How does he show anger?

6. What noises does a goat make? Do you understand what they mean?

7. Describe the goat, its looks and actions. Is the goat's tail short at first or does it have to be cut off like the lamb's tail? Where and how is goat's milk used? What kinds of cheese are made from it? For what is its skin used? Is its flesh ever eaten?

Everyone knows the gayety of young kids, which prompts them to cut the most amusing and burlesque capers. The goat is naturally capricious and inquisitive, and one might say crazy for every species of adventure. It positively delights in perilous ascensions. At times it will rear and threaten you with its head and horns, apparently, with the worst intentions, whereas it is usually an invitation to play. The bucks, however, fight violently with each other; they seem to have no consciousness of the most terrible blows. The ewes themselves are not exempt from this vice.

They know very well whether or not they have deserved punishment. Drive them out of the garden, where they are forbidden to go, with a whip and they will flee without uttering a sound; but strike them without just cause and they will send forth lamentable cries.

—CHARLES WILLIAM BURKETT "OUR DOMESTIC ANIMALS"

The Sheep

TEACHER'S STORY

"The earliest important achievement of ovine intelligence is to know whether its own notion or another's is most worth while, and if the other's, which one? Individual sheep have certain qualities, instincts, competences, but in the man-herded flocks these are superseded by something which I shall call the flock mind, though I cannot say very well what it is, except that it is less than the sum of all their intelligences. This is why there have never been any notable changes in the management of flocks since the first herder girt himself with a wallet of sheep-skin and went out of his cave-dwelling to the pastures."

—"The Flock," by Mary Austin

BOTH sheep and goats are at home on mountains, and sheep especially, thrive best in cool, dry locations. As wild animals, they were creatures of the mountain crag and chasm, although they frequented more open places than the mountain goats, and their wool was developed to protect them from the bitter cold of high altitudes. They naturally gathered in flocks, and sentinels were set to give warning of the approach of danger; as soon as the signal came, they made their escape, not in the straight away race like the deer, but in following the leader over rock, ledge and precipice to mountain fastnesses where wolf nor bear could

Cheviot ewe and lamb

follow. Thus, the instinct of following the leader blindly, came to be the salvation of the individual sheep.

The teeth of the sheep are like those of the goat, eight incisors below and none on the upper row, and six grinding teeth at the back of each side of each jaw. This arrangement of teeth on the small, delicate, pointed jaws enables the sheep to crop herbage where cattle would starve; it can cut the small grass off at its roots, and for this reason, where vast herds of sheep range, they leave a desert behind them. This fact brought about a bitter feud between the cattle and sheep men in the far West. In forests, flocks of sheep completely kill all underbrush, and now they are not permitted to run in government reserves.

The sheep's legs are short and delicate below the ankle. The upper portion is greatly developed to help the animal in leaping, a peculiarity to which we owe the "leg of lamb" as a table delicacy. The hoof is cloven, that is, the sheep walks upon two toes; it has two smaller toes above and behind these. There is a little gland between the front toes which secretes an oily substance, which perhaps serves in preventing the hoof from becoming too dry. The ears are large and are moved to catch better the direction of sound. The eyes are peculiar; in the sunlight the pupil is a mere slit, while the iris is yellow or brownish, but in the dark, even of the stable, the pupils enlarge, almost covering the eye. The ewes either lack horns or have small ones, but the horns of wild rams are large, placed at the side of the head and curled outward in a spiral. These horns are perhaps not so much for fighting the enemy as for rival rams. The ram can strike a hard blow with head and horns, coming at the foe head on, while the goat always strikes sidewise. So fierce is the blow of the angry sheep,

Feeding twins

that an ancient instrument of war was fashioned like a ram's head and used to knock down walls, and was called a battering ram. A sheep shows anger by stamping the ground with the front feet. The habit of rumination enables the sheep to feed in a flock and then retire to some place to rest and chew the cud, a performance peculiarly funny in the sheep.

Sheep under attack and danger are silent; ordinarily they keep up a constant, gentle bleating to keep each other informed of their whereabouts; they also give a peculiar call when water is discovered, and another to inform the flock that there is a stranger in the midst; they also give a peculiar bleat, when a snake or other enemy which they conquer, is observed. Their sense of smell is very acute. Mary Austin says, "Young lambs are principally legs, the connecting body being simply a contrivance for converting milk into more leg, so you understand how it is that they will follow the flock in two days and are able to take the trail in a fortnight, traveling four and five miles a day, falling asleep on their feet and tottering forward in the way."

The older lambs have games which they play untiringly, and which fit them to become active members of the flock; one, is the regular game of "Follow My Leader," each lamb striving to push ahead and attain the place of leader. In playing this the head lamb leads the chase over most

A pair of wild rams

difficult places, such as logs, stones and across brooks; thus is a training begun which later in life may save the flock. The other game is peculiar to stony pastures; a lamb climbs to the top of a boulder and its comrades gather around and try to butt it off; the one which succeeds in doing this, climbs the rock and is "it." This game leads to agility and sure-footedness. A lamb's tail is long and is most expressive of lambkin bliss, when feeding time comes; but, alas! it has to be cut off so that later it will not become matted with burrs and filth. In southern Russia there is a breed of sheep with large, flat, fat tails which are esteemed as a great table delicacy. This tail becomes so cumbersome that wheels are placed beneath it, so that it trundles along behind its owner.

We have a noble species of wild sheep in the Rocky Mountains which is likely to become extinct soon. The different breeds of domesticated sheep are supposed to have been derived from different wild species. Of the domesticated varieties, we have the Merinos which originated in Spain and which give beautiful, long, fine wool for our fabrics; but their flesh is not very attractive. The Merinos have wool on their faces and legs and have wrinkled skins. The English breeds of sheep have been especially developed for mutton, although their wool is valuable. Some of these, like the Southdown, Shropshire, and Dorset, give a medium length of wool, while the Cotswold has very long wool, the ewes having long strings of wool over their eyes in the fashion of "bangs."

The dog, as descended from the wolf, is the ancient enemy of sheep; and even now, after hundreds of years of domestication, some of our dogs will revert to savagery and chase and kill sheep. This, in fact, has been one of the great drawbacks to sheep raising in the Eastern United States. The collie, or sheep-dog, has been bred so many years as the special care-taker of sheep, that a beautiful relationship has been established between these dogs and their flocks. For instances of this, read the chapter on sheep-dogs in *A Country Reader*; "Wully" in *Wild Animals I Have Known*, and "Bob, Son of Battle."

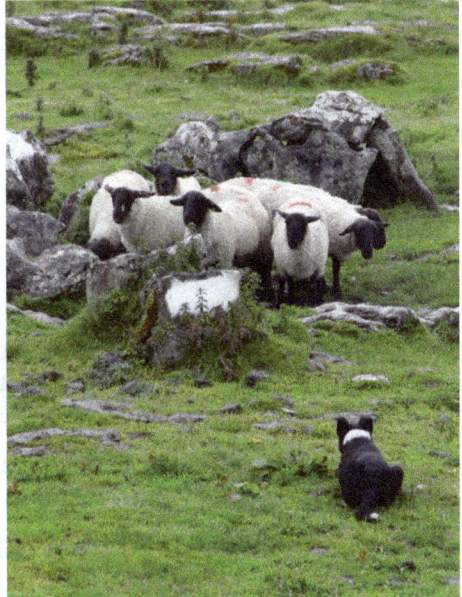
A sheep dog performing its duty

LESSON

Leading thought— Sheep live naturally in high altitudes. When attacked by enemies, they follow their leader over difficult and dangerous mountain places.

Method— The questions of this lesson should be given to the pupils and the observations should be made upon the sheep in pasture or stable. Much written work may be done in connection with this lesson. The following topics are suggested for themes: "The Methods by which Wool is Made into Cloth," "The Rocky Mountain Sheep," "The Sheep-herders of California and their Flocks," "The True Story of a Cosset Lamb."

Observations—

1. What is the chief character that separates sheep from other animals? What is the difference between wool and hair? Why is wool of special use to sheep in their native haunts? Is there any hair on sheep?

2. Where do the wild sheep live? What is the climate in these plac-

es? Does wool serve them well on this account? What sort of pasturage do sheep find on mountains? Could cows live where sheep thrive? Describe the sheep's teeth and how they are arranged to enable it to crop vegetation closely? What happens to the vegetation on the range, when a great flock of sheep passes over it? Why are sheep not allowed in our forest preserves?

3. What are the chief enemies of sheep in the wilderness? How do the sheep escape them? Describe the foot and leg of the sheep and explain how they help the animal to escape its enemies. We say of certain men that they "follow like a flock of sheep." Why do we make this comparison? What has this habit of following the leader to do with the escape of sheep from wolves and bears?

4. How do sheep fight? Do both rams and ewes have horns? Do they both fight? How does the sheep show anger? Give your experience with a cross cosset lamb.

5. Do you think that sheep can see and hear well? What is the position of the sheep's ears when it is peaceful? When there is danger? How do the sheep's eyes differ from those of the cow?

6. Does the sheep chew its cud like the cow? Describe the action as performed by the sheep. How is this habit of cud chewing of use to the wild sheep?

7. Describe a young lamb. Why has it such long legs? How does it use its tail to express joy? What happens to this tail later? What games have you seen lambs play? Tell all the stories of lambs that you know.

8. How much of sheep language do you understand? What is the use to the wild flock of the constant bleating?

9. For what purposes do we keep sheep? How many breeds of sheep do you know? What are the chief differences between the English breeds and the Merinos? Where and for what purposes is the milk of sheep used?

10. Have you ever seen a collie looking after a herd of sheep? If so, describe his actions. Did you ever know of dogs killing sheep? At what time of day or night was this done? Did you ever know of one dog attacking a flock of sheep alone? What is there in the dog's ancestry which makes two or three dogs, when hunting, give chase and attack sheep?

The Horse

"There was once a little animal no bigger than a fox,
And on five toes he scrambled over Tertiary rocks.
They called him Eohippus, and they called him very small,

And they thought him of no value when they thought of him at all.
Said the little Eohippus, I am going to be a horse!
And on my middle finger nails to run my earthly course!
I am going to have a flowing tail! I am going to have a mane!
And I am going to stand fourteen hands high on the Psychozooic plain!"
—Mrs. Stetson

IT was some millions of years ago, that Eohippus lived out in the Rocky Mountain Range; its fore feet had four toes and the splint of the fifth; the hind feet had three toes and the splint of the fourth. Eohippus was followed down the geologic ages by the Orohippus and the Mesohippus and various other hippuses, which showed in each age a successive enlargement and specialization of the middle toe and

A wild herd of horses

the minimizing and final loss of the others. This first little horse with many toes, lived when the earth was a damp, warm place and when animals needed toes to spread out to prevent them from miring in the mud. But as the ages went on, the earth grew colder and drier, and a long leg ending in a single hoof, was very serviceable in running swiftly over the dry plains; and according to the story read in the fossils of the rocks, our little American horses migrated to South America; and also trotted dry-shod over to Asia in the Mid-pleocine age, arriving there sufficiently early to become the companion of prehistoric man. In the meantime, horses were first hunted by savage man for their flesh, but were later ridden. At present, there are wild horses in herds on the plains of Tartary; and there are still sporadic herds of mustangs on the great plains of our own country, although for the most part, they are branded and belong to someone, even though they live like wild horses; these American wild horses are supposed to be descendents of those brought over centuries ago by the Spaniards. The Shetland ponies are also wild in the islands north of Scotland, and the zebras roam the plains of Africa, the most truly wild of all. In a state of wildness, there is always a stallion at the head of a herd of mares, and he has to win his position and keep it by superior strength and prowess. Fights between stallions are terrible to witness, and often result in the death of one of the participants. The horse is well armed for battle; his powerful teeth can inflict deep wounds and he can kick and strike hard with the front feet; still more efficient is the kick made with both hind feet while the weight of the body is borne on the front feet, and the head of the horse is turned so as to aim well the terrible blow. There are no wild beasts of prey which will not slink away to avoid a herd of horses. After attaining their growth in the herd with their mothers,

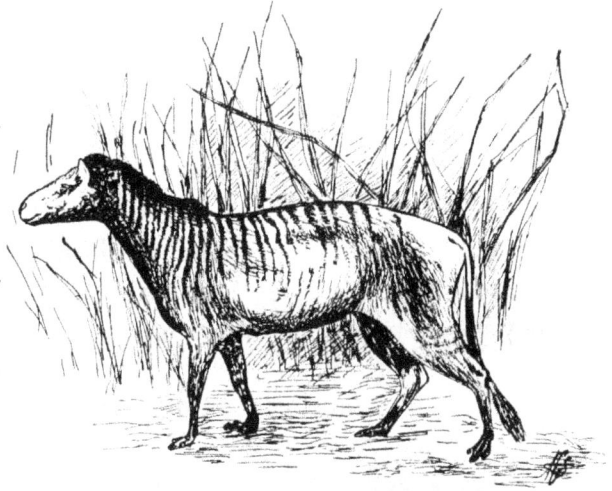

Four-toed horse of the Eocene period

the young males are forced by the leader to leave and go off by themselves; in turn, they must by their own strength and attractions, win their following of mares. However, there are times and places where many of these herds join, making large bands wandering together.

The length of the horse's leg was evidently evolved to meet the need for flight before fierce and swift enemies, on the great ancient plains. The one toe, with its strong, sharp hoof, makes a fit foot for such a long leg, since it strikes the ground with little waste of energy and is sharp enough not to slip, but it is not a good foot for marshy places; a horse will mire where a cow can pass in safety. The development of the middle toe into a hoof results in lifting the heel and wrist far up the leg, making them appear to be the knee and elbow, when compared with the human body.

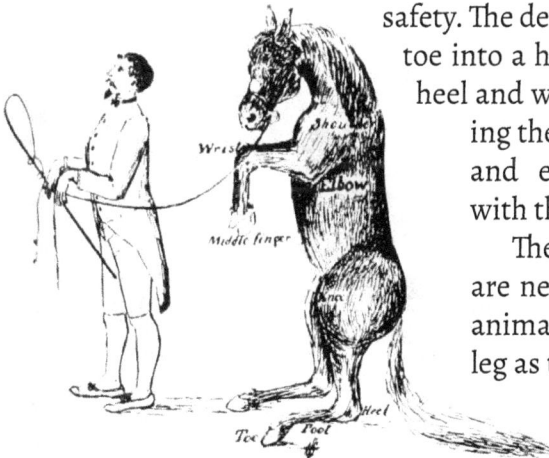

The length of neck and head are necessary in order that an animal, with such length of leg as the horse, may be able to graze. The head of the horse tells much of its disposition; a perfect head should be not too large, broad between the eyes and high between the ears, while below the eyes, it should be narrow. The ears, if lopped or turned back, denote a treacherous disposition. They should point upward or forward; the ears laid back is always a sign that the horse is angry; sensitive, quick-moving ears indicate a high-strung, sensitive animal. The eyes are placed so that the horse can see in front, at the side and behind, the last being necessary in order to aim a kick. Hazel eyes are usually preferred to dark ones, and they should be bright and prominent. The nostrils should be thin-skinned, wide-flaring and sensitive; as a wild animal, scent was one of the horse's chief aids in detecting the enemy. The lips should not be too thick and the lower jaw should be narrow where it joins the head.

The horse's teeth are peculiar; there are six incisors on both jaws; behind them, is a bare space called the bar, of which we have made use for placing the bit. Back of the bar, there are six molars or grinders on each side of each jaw. At the age of about three years, canine teeth or tushes appear behind the incisors; these are more noticeable in males, and never seem to be of much use. Thus, the horse has on each jaw, when full-grown, six incisors, two canines, and twelve molars, making forty teeth in all. The incisors are prominent and enable the horse to bite the grass more closely than can the cow. The horse, when chewing, does not have the sidewise motion of the jaws peculiar to the cow and sheep.

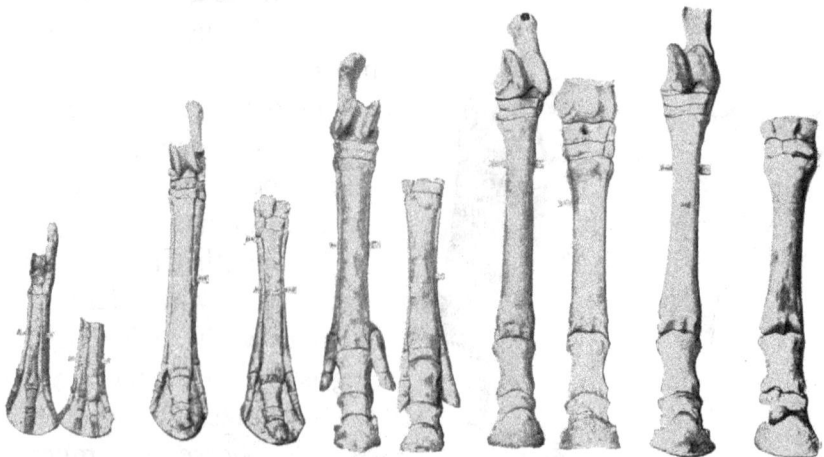

Hooves of horses from earliest ages to the present time, arranged in pairs, hind and front

The horse's coat is, when rightly cared for, glossy and beautiful; but if the horse is allowed to run out in the pasture all winter, the coat becomes very shaggy, thus reverting to the condition of wild horses which stand in need of a warmer coat for winter; the hair is

Draft horses

shed every year. The mane and the forelock are useful in protecting the head and neck from flies; the tail is also an efficient fly-brush. Although the mane and tail have thus a practical value, they add greatly to the animal's beauty. To dock a horse's tail as an ornament is as absurd as the sliced ears and welted cheeks of savages; and horses thus mutilated suffer greatly from the attacks of flies.

Owing to the fact that wild horses made swift flight from enemies, the colts could not be left behind at the mercy of wolves. Thus it is, the colt like the lamb, is equipped with long legs from the first, and can run very rapidly; as a runner, it could not be loaded with a big compound stomach full of food, like the calf, and therefore, must needs take its nourishment from the mother often. The colt's legs are so long that, in order to graze, it spreads the front legs wide apart in order that it may reach the grass with its mouth. When the colt or the horse lies down out of doors and in perfect freedom, it lies flat upon the side. In lying down, the hind quarters go first, and in rising, the front legs are thrust out first.

The horse has several natural gaits and some that are artificial. Its natural methods of progression are the walk, the trot, the amble, the gallop. When walking there are always two or more feet on the ground and the movement of the feet consists in placing successively the right hind foot, the right fore foot, left hind foot, left fore foot, right hind foot, etc. In trotting, each diagonal pair of legs is alternately lifted and thrust forward, the horse being unsupported twice during each

Saddled and ready to be ridden

stride. In ambling, the feet are moved as in the walk, only differing in that a hind foot or a fore foot is lifted from the ground, before its fellow fore foot or hind foot is set down. In a canter, the feet are landed on the ground in the same sequence as a walk but much more rapidly; and in the gallop, the spring is made from the fore foot and the landing is on the diagonal hind foot and, just before landing, the body is in the air and the legs are all bent beneath it.

An excellent horseman once said to me, "The whip may teach a horse to obey the voice, but the voice and hand control the well-broken horse," and this epitomizes the best horse training. He also said, "The horse knows a great deal, but he is too nervous to make use of his knowledge when he needs it most. It is the horse's feelings that I rely on. He always has the use of his feelings and the quick use of them." It is a well-known fact that those men who whip and scold and swear at their horses, are meantime showing to the world that they are fools in this particular business. Many of the qualities which we do not like in our domesticated horses, were most excellent and useful when the horses were wild; for instance, the habit of shying was the wild horse's method of escaping the crouching foe in the grass. This habit as well as many others is best controlled by the voice of the driver instead of a blow from the whip.

Timothy hay, or hay mixed with clover, form good, bulky food for the horse, and oats and corn are the best concentrated food. Oats are best for driving-horses and corn for the working team. Dusty hay should not be fed to a horse; but if unavoidable, it should always be dampened before feeding. A horse should be fed with regularity, and should not be used for a short time after having eaten. If the horse is not warm, it should be watered before feeding, and in the winter the water should have the chill taken off. The frozen bit should be warmed before being placed in the horse's mouth; if anyone doubts the wisdom of this, let him put a frozen piece of steel in his own mouth. The tight-drawn, cruel use of the

The Godolphin Arabian

over check-rein should not be permitted, although a moderate check is often needed and is not cruel. When the horse is sweating, it should be blanketed immediately if hitched outside in cold weather; but in the barn, the blanket should not be put on until the perspiration has stopped steaming. The grooming of a horse is a part of its rights, and its legs should receive more attention during this process than its body, a fact not always well understood.

The breeds of horses may always be classified more or less distinctly as follows: Racers or thoroughbreds; the saddle-horse, or hunter; the coach-horse; the draft-horse and the pony. For a description of breeds see dictionaries or cyclopedias. Of the draft-horses, the Percherons, Shires and Clydesdales are most common; of the carriage and coach-horses, the English hackney and the French and German coach-horses are famed examples. Of the roadster breeds, the American trotter, the American saddle-horse and the English thoroughbred are most famous.

LESSON

Leading thought— The horse as a wild animal depended largely upon its strength and fleetness to escape its enemies, and these two qualities have made it of greatest use to man.

Method— Begin this study of the horse with the stories of wild horses. "The Pacing Mustang" in Wild Animals I Have Known, is an excellent story to show the habits of the herds of wild horses; Chapter first in A Country Reader and the story of horses in Life of Animals are ex-

A shetland pony

cellent as a basis for study. Before beginning actual study of the domestic horses, ask for oral or written English exercises descriptive of the lives of the wild horses. Get Remington's pictures illustrating the wild horses of America. After the interest has been thus aroused the following observations may be suggested, a few at a time, to be made incidentally in the street or in the stable.

Observations—

1. Compare the length of the legs of the horse with its height. Has any other domestic animal legs as long in proportion? What habits of the ancestral wild horses led to the development of such long legs? Do you think the length of the horse's neck and head correspond to the length of its legs? Why?

2. Study the horse's leg and foot. The horse walks on one toe. Which toe do you think it is? What do we call the toe-nail of the horse? What advantage is this sort of a foot to the horse? Is it best fitted for running on dry plains or for marshy land? Does the hoof grow as our nails do? Do you know whether there were ever any horses with three toes or four toes on each foot? Make a sketch of the horse's front and hind leg and label those places which correspond to our wrist, elbow, shoulder, hand, heel, knee and hip.

3. Where are the horse's ears placed on the head? How do they move? Do they flap back and forth like the cow's ears when they are moved, or do they turn as if on a pivot? What do the following different positions of the horse's ears indicate: When lifted and pointing forward? When thrown back? Can you tell by the action of the ears whether a horse is nervous and high-strung or not?

4. What is the color of the horse's eyes? The shape of the pupil?

What advantage does the position of the eyes on the head give to the wild horse? Why do we put blinders on a horse? Can you tell by the expression of the eye the temper of the horse?

The eye of a horse

5. Look at the mouth and nose. Are the nostrils large and flaring? Has the horse a keen sense of smell? Are the lips thick or thin? When taking sugar from the hand, does the horse use teeth or lips?

6. Describe the horse's teeth. How many front teeth? How many back teeth? Describe the bar where the bit is placed. Are there any canine teeth? If so, where? Do you know how to tell a horse's age by its teeth? (See Elements of Agriculture, Warren, page 304, and The Horse, Roberts, page 246.) Can a horse graze the grass more closely than a cow? Why? When it chews does it move the jaws sidewise like the cow? Why? Why did the wild horses not need to develop a cud-chewing habit?

7. What is the nature of the horse's coat in summer? If the horse runs in the pasture all winter, how does its coat change? When does the horse shed its coat? What is the use of the horse's mane, forelock and tail? Do you think it is treating the horse well to dock its tail?

8. Why do colts need to be so long-legged? How does a colt have to place its front legs in order to reach down and eat the grass? Does the colt need to take its food from the mother often? How does it differ from the calf in this respect? How has this difference of habit resulted in a difference of form in the calf and colt?

9. When the horse lies down which part goes down first? When getting up which rises first? How does this differ from the method of the cow? When the horse lies down to sleep does it have its legs partially under it like the cow?

10. In walking which leg moves first? Second? Third? Fourth? How

many gaits has the horse? Describe as well as you can all of these gaits. (See pictures illustrating the word "movement" in the Standard Dictionary.)

11. Make a sketch of a horse showing the parts. (See Webster's Unabridged). When we say a horse is fourteen hands high what do we mean?

12. In fighting, what weapons does the horse use and how?

13. In training a horse, should the voice or the whip be used the most? What qualities should a man have to be a good horse trainer? Why is shying a good quality in wild horses? How should it be dealt with in the domestic horse?

14. What sort of feed is best for the horse? How and when should the horse be watered? Should the water be warmed in cold weather? Why? Should the bit be warmed in winter before putting it in a horse's mouth? Why? Should a tight over check-rein be used when driving? Why? When the horse has been driven until it is sweating what are the rules for blanketing it when hitched out of doors and when hitched in the barn? What is your opinion of a man who lets his horse stand waiting in the cold, unblanketed in the village street. If horses were kept out of doors all the time would this treatment be so cruel and dangerous? Why? Why should dusty hay be dampened before it is fed to a horse? Why should a horse

be groomed? Which should receive the most attention, the legs or the body?

15. How many breeds of horses do you know? What is the use of each? Describe as well as you can the characteristics of the following breeds: The thoroughbred, the hackney, and other coach-horses; the American trotter, the Percheron, the Clydesdale.

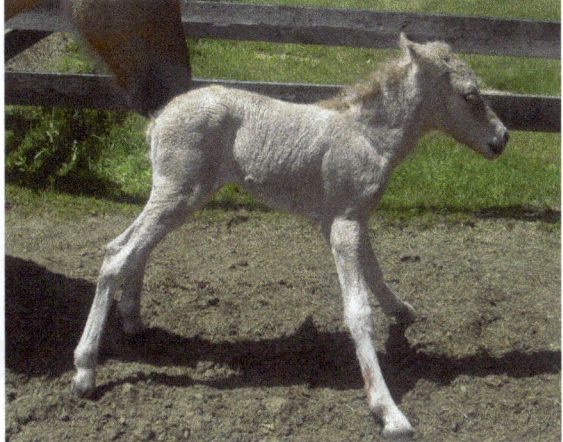
A new foal

16. Write English themes on the following subjects: "The Prehistoric Horses of America," "The Arabian Horse and Its Life With Its Master," "The Bronchos and Mustangs of the West," "The Wild Horses of Tartary," "The Zebras of Africa," "The Shetland Ponies and the Islands on Which They Run Wild."

Supplementary reading—*The Horse*, Roberts; *Elements of Agriculture*, Warren; *Life of Animals*, Cram; *Neighbors with Claws and Hoofs*; *A Country Reader*; *Agriculture for Beginners*; *Black Beauty*; *John Brent*, by Theodore Withrop; *Half Hours with Mammals*, Holder; *Chapters on Animals*, Hammerton; "Kaweah's Run" in *Claws and Hoofs*.

Many horses shy a good deal at objects they meet on the road. This mostly arises from nervousness, because the objects are not familiar to them. Therefore, to cure the habit, you must get your horse accustomed to what he sees, and so give him confidence. . . . . Be careful never to stop a horse that is drawing a vehicle or load in the middle of a hill, except for a rest; and if for a rest, draw him across the hill and place a big stone behind the wheel, so that the strain on the shoulder may be eased. Unless absolutely necessary never stop a horse on a hill or in a rut, so that when he starts again it means a heavy tug. Many a horse has been made a jibber and his temper spoilt by not observing this rule.

—H. B. M. Buchanan "A Country Reader"

The original wild cattle of America

Cattle

TEACHER'S STORY

THAT in numbers there is safety, is a basic principle in the lives of wild cattle, probably because their chief enemies, the wolves, hunted in packs. It has often been related that, when the herd is attacked by wolves, the calves are placed at the center of the circle made by the cattle, standing with heads out and horns ready for attack from every quarter. But when a single animal, like a bear or tiger, attacks any of the herd, they all gather around it in a narrowing circle of clashing horns, and many of these great beasts of prey have thus met their death. The cow is as formidable as the bull to the enemy, since her horns are strong and sharp and she tosses her victim, unless it is too large. The heavy head, neck and short massive horns of the bull, are not so much for defence against enemies as against rival bulls. The bull not only tosses and gores his victim, but kneels or tramples upon it. Both have effective weapons of defence in the hind feet, which kick powerfully. The buffalo bull of India will attack a tiger single handed, and usually successfully. It is a strange thing that all cattle are driven mad by the smell of blood, and weird stories are told of the stampeding of herds from this cause, on the plains of our great West.

Cattle are essentially grass and herbage eaters, and their teeth are peculiarly arranged for this. There are eight front teeth on the lower jaw, and a horny pad opposite them on the upper jaw. Back of these on each jaw there is a bare place and six grinding teeth on each side. As a cow crops the herbage, her head is moved up and down to aid in severing the leaves, and the peculiar sound of the tearing of the leaves thus

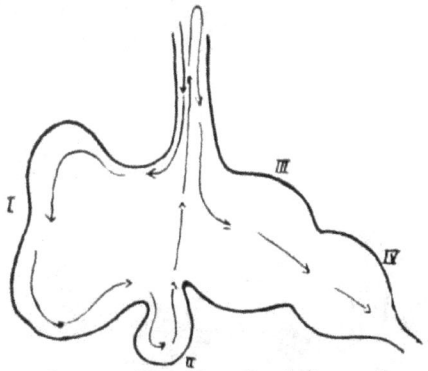

Course of Food in a Cow's Stomach
I. ruminant stomach;
II. where the cud-balls are formed;
III. and IV. true stomachs.

made is not soon forgotten by those who have heard it. In the wild or domesticated state the habit of cud-chewing is this: The cattle graze in mornings and evenings, swallowing the food as fast as cropped, and storing it in their ruminating stomachs. During the heat of the day, they move to the shade, preferably to the shady banks of streams, and there in quiet the food is brought up, a small portion at a time, and chewed with a peculiar sidewise movement of the jaws and then swallowed, passing to the true stomach. There is probably no more perfect picture of utter contentment, than a herd of cows chewing their cuds in the shade, or standing knee-deep in the cool stream on a summer's day. The cattle in a herd when grazing, keep abreast and move along, heads in the same direction.

Connected with the grazing habit, is that of the hiding of the new-born calf by its mother; the young calf is a wabbly creature and ill-fitted for a long journey; so the mother hides it, and there it stays "frozen" and will never stir unless actually touched. As the mother is obliged to be absent for some time grazing with the herd, the calf is obliged to go without nourishment for a number of hours, and so it is provided with a large compound stomach which, if filled twice per day, suffices to insure health and growth. The cow, on the other hand, giving her milk out only twice per day, needs a large udder in which to store it. The size of the udder is what has made the cow useful to us as a milch animal.

Cows in pasture

A fine cow is a beautiful creature, her soft yellow skin beneath the sleek coat of short hair, the well proportioned body, the mild face, crowned with spreading, polished horns and illuminated with large gentle eyes, are all elements of beauty which artists have recognized, especially those of the Dutch school. The ancients also admired bovine eyes, and called their most beautiful goddess the ox-eyed Juno.

The cow's ears can be turned in any direction, and her sense of hearing is keen; so is her sense of smell, aided by the moist, sensitive skin of the nose; she always sniffs danger and also thus tests her food. Although a cow if well kept has a sleek coat, when she is allowed to run out of doors during the winter, her hair grows long and shaggy as a protection. The cow walks on two toes, or, as we say, has a split hoof. She has two lesser toes above and behind the hoofs which we call dew-claws. The part of her leg which seems at first glance to be her knee, is really her wrist or ankle. Although short-legged, the cow is a good runner, as those who have chased her can bear witness. She can walk, gallop and has a pacing trot; she is a remarkable jumper, often taking a fence like a deer; she also has marvelous powers as a swimmer, a case being on record where a cow swam five miles. But a cow would be illy equipped for comfort if it were not for her peculiar tail, which is made after the most approved pattern of fly-brushes, and is thus used. Woe betide the fly she hits with it, if the blow is as efficient as that which she incidentally bestows on the head of the milker. It is to get rid of flies, that the cattle, and especially the buffaloes,

A highland longhorn bull

wallow in the mud, and thus coat themselves with a fly-proof armor.

There is a fairly extensive range of emotions expressed in cattle language, from the sullen bellow of the angry animal to the lowing which is the call of the herd, and the mooing which is meant for the calf; and there are many other bellowings and mutterings which we can partially understand.

Every herd of cows has its leader, which has won the position by fair fight. Add a new cow to the herd, and there is at once a trial of strength, to adjust her to her proper place; and in a herd of cows, the leader leads; she goes first and no one may say her nay. In fact, each member of the herd has her place in it; and that is why it is so easy to teach cows each to take her own stanchion in the stable. In a herd of forty cows which I knew, each cow took her stanchion, no matter in what order she happened to enter the stable.

A cow at play is a funny sight; her tail is lifted aloft like a pennant and she kicks as lightly as if she were made of rubber. She is also a surefooted beast, as anyone can attest who has seen her running down the rocky mountain sides of the Alps, at a headlong pace and never making a mistake. In lying down, the cow first kneels with the front legs, or rather drops on her wrists, and then the hind quarters go down, and then the front follow. She does not lie flat on her side when resting, like the horse when at ease, but with her legs partially under her. In getting up, she rests upon her wrists and then lifts the hind quarters.

THE USEFULNESS OF CATTLE

A Jersey cow. Notice the characteristic white ring around its black nose

WHEN man emerged from the savage state, his first step toward civilization was domesticating wild animals and training them for his own use. During the nomad stage, when tribes wandered over the face of the earth, they took their cattle along. From the first, these animals have been used in three capacities: First, for carrying burdens and as draught animals; second, as meat; third, as givers of milk. They were also used in the earlier ages as sacrifices to the various deities, and in Egypt, some were held as sacred.

As beasts of burden and draft animals, oxen are still used in many parts of the United States. For logging, especially in pioneer days, oxen were far more valuable than horses. They are patient and will pull a few inches at a time, if necessary, a tedious work which the nervous horse refuses to endure. Cows, too, have been used as draft animals, and are so used in China today, where they do most of the plowing; in these oriental countries milk is not consumed to any extent, so the cow is kept for the work she can do. In ancient times in the East, white oxen formed a part of royal processions.

Because of two main uses of cattle by civilized man, he has bred them in two directions; one for producing beef, and one for milk. The beef cattle are chiefly Aberdeen-Angus, Galloway, Short-horn or Durham, and Hereford; the dairy breeds are the Jersey, Guernsey, Ayrshire, Holstein-Frisian and Brown Swiss. The beef animal is, in cross-section, approximately like a brick set sidewise. It should be big and full across the loins and back, the shoulders and hips covered heavily with flesh, the legs stout, the neck thick and short, and the face short; the line of the back is straight, and the stomach line parallel with it. Very different is the appearance of the milch cow. Her body is oval, instead of being approximately square in cross-section. The outline of her back is not straight, but sags in front of the hips, which are prominent and bony. The shoulders have little flesh on them; and if looked at from above, her body is wedge-shaped, widening from shoulders backward. The stomach line is not parallel

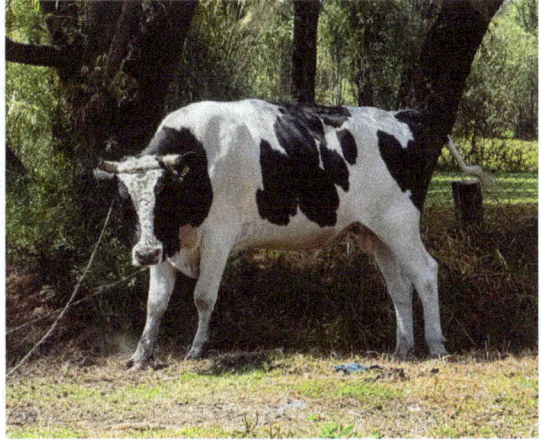

A Holstein bull

with the back bone, but slants downward from the shoulder to the udder. The following are the points that indicate a good milch cow: Head high between the eyes, showing large air passages and indicating strong lungs. Eyes clear, large, and placid, indicating good disposition. Mouth large, with a muscular lower jaw, showing ability to chew efficiently and rapidly. Neck, thin and fine, showing veins through the skin. Chest, deep and wide, showing plenty of room for heart and lungs. Abdomen, large but well supported, and increasing in size toward the rear. Ribs, well spread, not meeting the spine like the peak of a roof, but the spine must be prominent, revealing to the touch the separate vertebrae. Hips, much broader than the shoulders. Udder, large, the four quarters of equal size, and not fat; the "milk veins" which carry the blood from the udder should be large and crooked, passing into the abdomen through large openings. Skin, soft, pliable, and covered with fine, oily hair. She should have good digestion and great powers of assimilation. The milch cow is a milk-making machine, and the more fuel (food) she can use, the greater her production.

The physiological habits of the beef and milch cattle have been changed as much as their structure. The food given to the beef cow goes to make flesh; while that given to the milch cow goes to make milk, however abundant her food. Of course, there are all grades between the beef and the milch types, for many farmers use dual herds for both. However, if a farmer is producing milk, it pays him well to get the best possible machine to make it, and that is always a cow of the right type.

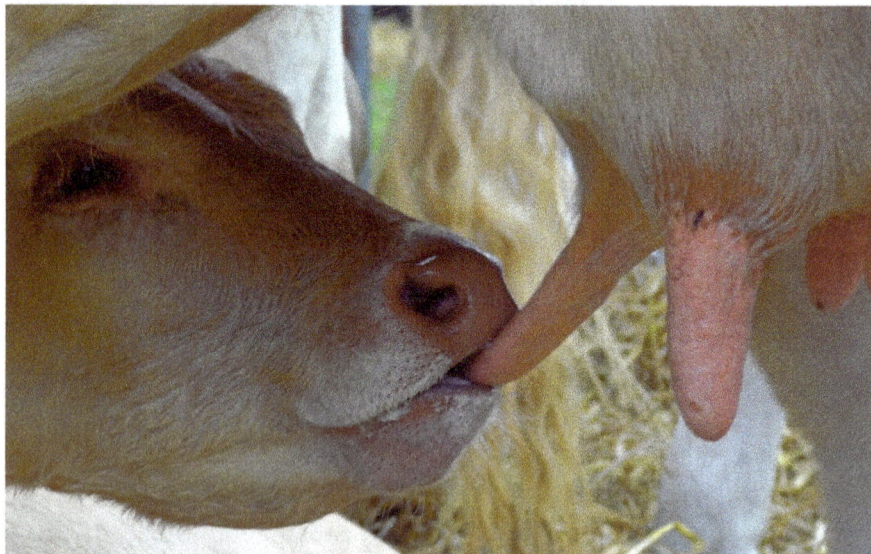

A GEOGRAPHY LESSON

ALL the best breeds of cattle have been evolved in the British Isles and in Europe north of Italy and west of Russia. All our domesticated cattle were developed from wild cattle of Europe and Asia. The cattle which roam in our rapidly narrowing grazing lands of the far West are European cattle. America had no wild cattle except the bison. In geography supplementary readers, read about Scotland, England, the Channel Islands, the Netherlands, France and Switzerland and the different kinds of cattle developed in these countries; for example, "A Holland Dairy," in Northern Europe, Ginn & Co.

HOW TO PRODUCE GOOD MILK

THERE are three main ingredients of milk—fat, curd and ash. The fat is for the purpose of supplying the animal with fat and we make it into butter; the curd supplies muscle, or the lean meat of the animal, and is the main ingredient of cheese, although cheese to be good should contain a full amount of butter fat; the ash, which may be seen as residue when milk is evaporated, builds up the bone of the animal. The best butter cows are those which give a larger per cent of fat and a small per cent of curd, like the Jerseys; the best cheese cows are those

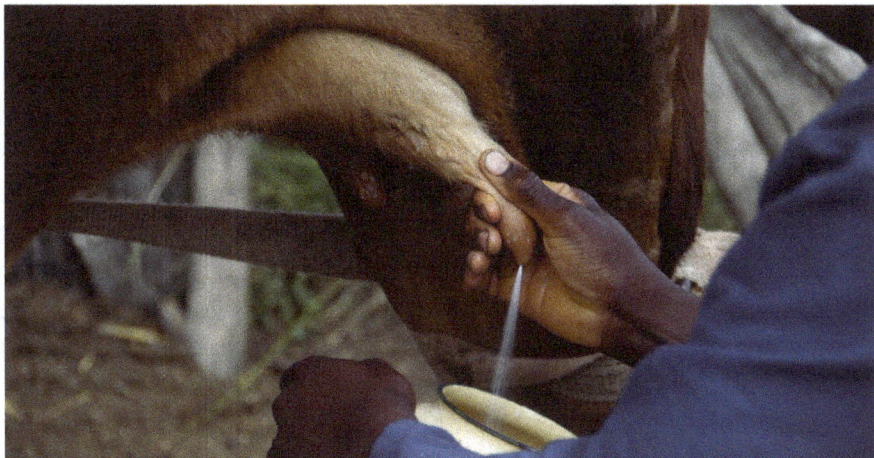
Milking a cow

which give a fair per cent of fat and a larger yield of curd, like the Ayr-shire and Holstein.

A cow for producing cheese, is not profitable, unless she gives seven thousand pounds of milk per year; a butter cow, a Jersey for instance, should produce five thousand pounds of milk per year to be really profitable.

The stable where milch cows are kept should be thoroughly cleaned before each milking, and should be swept each day; the cows' udders should be brushed, and the milkers should wear clean aprons and should wash their hands before milking. Milk should never be strained in the barn, but in some place where the air is fresh. If milk is perfectly clean, it will keep sweet much longer; sterilized milk put in bottles will keep sweet for weeks and even months. Loud talking should not be permitted in the stables while the cows are being milked, and each cow should be milked by the same person for the entire season.

Milk to be legally sold in New York State must possess three per cent of butter fat. For upper grades or first year work in the high school, there could not be a more profitable exercise than teaching the pupils the use of the Babcock milk tester.

The Care of the Milch Cow

THE importance cannot be over-estimated of teaching the pupils in rural districts, the proper care of milch cattle for the production of milk. The milch cow is a perfect machine, and should be regarded as such in producing milk. First, she should have plenty of food of the right kind, that is, a well-balanced ration. Second, she should have a warm, clean stable and be supplied with plenty of good, fresh air. A cold stable makes it necessary to provide much more food for the cow; a case on record shows that when a barn was opened up in cold weather for necessary repairing, the amount of milk from the cows stabled in it, decreased ten per cent, in twenty-four hours. There should be a protected place for drinking, if the cattle must be turned out of the barn for water in winter; it is far better to have the water piped into the barn, although the herd should be given a few hours each day in the open air. A dog should never be used for driving cows. To be profitable, a cow should give milk ten months of the year at least. Calves should be dehorned when they are a few days old by putting caustic potash on the budding horns, thus obviating the danger of damaging the cow by dehorning.

In a properly run dairy, a pair of scales stands near the can for receiving the milk; and as the milk from each cow is brought in, it is weighed and the amount set down opposite the cow's name on a "milk sheet," that is tacked on the wall, near by. At the end of each week, the figures on the milk sheet are added, and the farmer knows just how much milk each cow is giving him, and whether there are any in the herd which are not paying their board.

References— *Elements of Agriculture*, Warren; *Agriculture for Beginners*, Burkett, Stevens and Hill, p. 216; *First Principles of Agriculture*, Vorhees, p. 117; *Elements of Agriculture*, Sever, p. 57; *Elements of Agriculture*, Shepperd, chapters 15 and 22; *First Principles of Agriculture*, Goff and Maine, p. 154; *Agriculture Through the Laboratory*, School and Garden, Jackson and Dougherty, chapter 8; *The Dairy Herd*, Farmers' Bulletin No. 55, U. S. Dept. of Agr.; *Care of Milk on the Farm*, Farmers' Bulletin No. 63, U. S. Dept. of Agr.

Black Angus cows grazing
LESSON

Leading thought— Certain characteristics, which enable the cow to live successfully as a wild animal, have rendered her of great use to us as a domestic animal.

Method— Begin the lesson with leading the pupils to understand the peculiar adaptation of cattle for success, as wild animals. This will have to be done largely by reading and asking for oral or written work on the following topics: "The Aurochs," "Wild Cattle of the Scottish Highlands," "The Buffaloes of the Orient," "The American Bison," "The Cow-boys of the West and their Work with their Herds," "The Breeds of Beef Cattle, Where they Came From, and Where Developed," "The Breeds of Milch Cattle, their Origin and Names." The following questions may be given out a few at a time and answered as the pupils have opportunity for observation.

Observations—

1. What are the characteristics of a fine cow? Describe her horns, ears, eyes, nose and mouth. Do you think she can hear well? What is the attitude of her ears when she is listening? Do you think she has a keen sense of smell? Is her nose moist? Is her hair long or short? Smooth or rough?

2. The cow walks on two toes. Can you see any other toes which she does not walk on? Why is the cow's foot better adapted than that of the horse, to walk in mud and marshes? What do we call the two hind toes which she does not walk on? Can you point out on the cow's leg those parts which correspond with our elbow, wrist, knee and ankle? Is the cow a good runner? Is she a good jumper? Can she swim?

3. For what use was the cow's tail evidently intended? How do the wild buffalos and bisons get rid of attacks of flies?

4. How much of cattle language do you understand? How does the cow express pleasure? Lonesomeness? Anger? How does the bull express anger? What does the calf express with the voice?

5. Is there always a leader in a herd of cows? Do certain cows of the herd always go first and others last? Do the cows readily learn to take each her own place in the stable? How is leadership of the herd attained? Describe cattle at play.

6. At what time of day do cattle feed in the pasture? When and where do they chew the cud? Do they stand or lie to do this? Describe how a cow lies down and gets up.

7. How do wild cattle defend themselves from wolves? From bears or other solitary animals?

8. For what purposes were cattle first domesticated? For how many purposes do we rear cattle today?

9. Name and give brief descriptions of the different breeds of cattle with which you are familiar. Which of these are beef and which milch types?

10. What are the distinguishing points of a good milch cow? Of a good beef animal? What does the food do for each of these? Which part of the United States produces most beef cattle? Which the most milch cattle?

11. What do we mean by a balanced ration? Do you know how to compute one? What is the advantage of feeding cattle a balanced ration?

12. How many pounds of milk should a dairy cow produce in a year to be profitable if the product is cheese? If the product is butter? Why this discrepancy? What must be the per cent of butter fat in milk to make it legally salable in your state? How many months of the year

A young calf

should a good cow give milk?

13. Why should a cow be milked always by the same person? Does the milker always sit on the same side? Why should loud talking and other noise at milking time be avoided? Should a dog be used in driving dairy cows? Why?

14. Why is a cool draughty barn an expensive place in which to keep cattle? Why is a barn, not well-ventilated, a danger?

15. Why and where is the dehorning of cattle practiced? When and how should a calf be dehorned?

16. Why should milk not be strained in the barn? Why is it profitable for the dairy farmer to keep his stable clean and to be cleanly in the care of milk? How does the food of cows affect the flavor of the milk? Why should a farmer keep a record of the number of pounds of milk which each cow in his dairy gives each day?

17. For what are oxen used? Wherein are they superior to horses as draft animals? Do you know of any place where oxen are used as riding animals?

18. How many industries are dependent upon cattle?

19. Give oral or written exercises on the following themes: "How the Best Butter is Made;" "The Use of Bacteria in Butter;" "How Dairy Cheese is Made;" "How Fancy Cheeses are Made."

All lined up at the milk-bar

The Pig

TEACHER'S STORY

"I wander through the underbresh,
Where pig tracks pintin' to'rds the crick,
Is picked and printed in the fresh
Black bottom-lands, like wimmen prick
Their pie-crust with a fork."

—RILEY

By a forest law of William the First of England in the eleventh century, it was ordained that any that were found guilty of killing the stag or the roebuck or the wild boar should have their eyes put out. This shows that the hunting of the wild boar in England was considered a sport of gentlemen in an age when nothing was considered sport unless it was dangerous. The wild hog of Europe is the ancestor of our common domesticated breeds, although the Chinese domesticated their own wild species, even before the dawn of history.

The wild hog likes damp situations where it may wallow in the water and mud; but it also likes to have, close by, woods, thicket, or underbrush, to which it can

A family of wild pigs

retire for rest and also when in danger. The stiff, bristling hairs which cover its thick skin are a great protection when it is pushing through thorny thickets. When excited or angry, these bristles rise and add to the fury of its appearance. Even in our own country the wild hogs of the South whose ancestors escaped from domestication have reverted to their original savagery, and are dangerous when infuriated. The only recorded instance when our great national hunter, Theodore Roosevelt, was forced ignominiously to climb a tree, was after he had emptied his rifle into a herd of "javelins," as the wild pigs of Texas are called; the javelins are the peccaries, which are the American representatives of the wild hog.

That the hog has become synonymous with filth is the result of the influence of man upon this animal, for of all animals, the pig is naturally the neatest, keeping its bed clean, often in the most discouraging and ill-kept pens. The pig is sparsely clothed with bristles and hairs, which yield it no protection from the attacks of flies and other insects. Thus it is that the pig, in order to rid itself of these pests, has learned to wallow in the mud. However, this is in the nature of a mud bath, and is for the purpose of keeping the body free from vermin. The wild hogs of India make for themselves grass huts, thatched above and with doors at the sides, which shows that the pig, if allowed to care for itself, understands well the art of nest building. One of the most interesting things about a pig is its nose; this is a fleshy disc with nostrils in it and is a most sensitive organ of feeling; it can select grain from chaff, and yet it is so strong that it can root up the ground in search for food. "Root" is a pig word, and was evidently coined to describe the act

Pigs have an amazing sense of smell

of the pig when digging for roots; the pig's nose is almost as remarkable as the elephant's trunk, and the pig's sense of smell is very keen; it will follow a track almost as well as a dog. There are more instances than one of a pig being trained as a pointer for hunting birds, and showing a keener sense of smell and keener intelligence in this capacity than do dogs. French pigs are taught to hunt for truffles, which are fungi growing on tree roots, a long way below the surface of the ground; the pig detects their presence through the sense of smell.

The pig has a full set of teeth, having six incisors, two canines, and seven grinding teeth on each jaw; although in some cases there are only four incisors on the upper jaw. A strange thing about a pig's teeth is the action of the upper canines, or tushes, which curve upward instead of downward; the lower canines grind up against them, and are thus sharpened. The females have no such development of upper tushes as do the males; these tushes, especially the upper ones, are used as weapons; with them, the wild boar slashes out and upward, inflicting terrible wounds, often disabling horses and killing men. Professor H. F. Button describes the fighting of hogs thus: "To oppose the terrible weapons of his rival, the boar has a shield of skin over his neck and shoulders, which may become two inches thick, and so hard as to defy a knife. When two of these animals fight, each tries to keep the tushes of his opponent against the shield, and to get his own tushes under the belly or flank of the other. Thus, each goes sidewise or in circles, which has given rise to the expression, 'to go sidewise like a hog to war.'"

A piglet

When, as a small girl, I essayed the difficult task of working buttonholes, I was told if I did not set my stitches more closely together, my buttonhole would look like a pig's eye, a remark which made me observant of that organ ever after. But though the pig's eyes are small, they certainly gleam with intelligence, and they take in all that is going on which may in any way affect his pigship.

The pig is the most intelligent of all the farm animals, if it is only given a chance; it has excellent memory and can be taught tricks readily; it is affectionate and will follow its master around like a dog. Anyone who has seen a trained pig at a show picking out cards and counting must grant that it has brains. We stuff it so with fattening food, however, that it does not have a chance to use its brain, except now and then when it breaks out of the sty and we try to drive it back. Under these circumstances, we grant the pig all the sagacity usually imputed to the one who once possessed swine and drove them into the sea. Hunters of wild hogs proclaim that they are full of strategy and cunning, and are exceedingly fierce.

The head of the wild hog is wedge-shaped with pointed snout, and this form enables the animal to push into the thick underbrush along the river banks whenever it is attacked. But civilization has changed this bold profile of the head, so that now in many breeds there is a

Playing in the trough

hollow between the snout and eyes, giving the form which we call "dished." Some breeds have sharp, forward-opening ears, while others have ears that lop. The wild pig of Europe and Asia has large, open ears extending out wide and alert on each side of the head.

The covering of the pig is a thick skin beset with bristling hairs; when the hog is excited, the bristles rise and add to the fury of its appearance. The bristles aid in protecting the animal when it is pushing through thorny thickets. The pig's querly tail is merely an ornament, although the tail of the wart hog of Africa, if pictures may be relied upon, might be used in a limited fashion as a fly-brush.

When the pig is allowed to roam in the woods, it lives on roots, nuts, and especially acorns and beech nuts; in the autumn it becomes very fat through feeding upon the latter. The mast-fed bacon of the semi-wild hogs of the southern states is considered the best of all. But almost anything, animal or vegetable, that comes in its way is eaten by the hog, and it has been long noted that the hog has done good sendee on our frontier as a killer of rattlesnakes. The pig is well fitted for locomotion on either wet or dry soil, for the two large hoofed toes enable it to walk well on dry ground and the two hind toes, smaller and higher up, help to sustain it on marshy soil. Although the pig's legs are short, it is a swift runner unless it is too fat. The razor-backs of the South are noted for their fleetness.

We understand somewhat the pig's language: the constant grunting, which is a sound that keeps the pig herd together, the complaining squeal of hunger, the satisfied grunt signifying enjoyment of food, the squeal of terror when seized, and the nasal growl when fighting. But there is much more to the pig's conversation than this; I knew a certain lady, a lover of animals, who once undertook to talk pig language as best she could imitate it, to two of her sows when they were engaged in eating. They stopped eating, looked at each other a moment and forthwith began fighting, each evidently attributing the lady's remark to the other, and obviously it was of an uncomplimentary character.

The pig's ability to take on fat was evidently a provision, in the wild state, for storing up from mast fat that should help sustain the animal during the hardships of winter; and this characteristic is what makes swine useful for our own food. Pigs, to do best, should be allowed to have pasture and plenty of fresh green food. Their troughs should be kept clean and they should have access to ashes, and above all, they should have plenty of pure water; and as the pig does not perspire freely, access to water where it can take its natural mud baths helps to keep the body cool and the pig healthy in hot weather.

The breeds of hogs most common in America are the Berkshire, which are black and white markings, and have ears extending erect; the Poland China, which are black and white with drooping ears; the Duroc-Jersey, which are red or chestnut with drooping ears; the Yorkshire and Cheshire, which are white with erect ears; and the Chester White, which are white with drooping ears. The Poland China and Duroc-Jersey are both pure American breeds.

SUGGESTED READING *Baby Animals on the Farm*, by Kate E. Agnew and Margaret Coble; *Farm Animals*, by James G. Lawson; *Mother Nature Series*, by Fannie W. Dunn and Eleanor Troxell, Book 1, Baby Animals; *The Pet Book*, by Anna B. Comstock.

LESSON

Leading thought — The pig is something more than a source of pork. It is a sagacious animal and naturally cleanly in its habits when not made prisoner by man.

Method — The questions in this lesson may be given to the pupils a few at a time, and those who have access to farms or other places where pigs are kept may make the observations, which should be discussed when they are given to the class. Supplementary reading should be given the pupils, which may inform them as to the habits and peculiarities of the wild hogs. Theodore Roosevelt's experience in hunting the wart hog in Africa will prove interesting reading.

Observations — 1. How does the pig's nose differ from that of other animals? What is it used for besides for smelling? Do you think the pig's sense of smell is very keen? Why do pigs root?

2. Describe the pig's teeth. For what are they fitted? What are the tushes for? Which way do the upper tushes turn? How do wild hogs use their tushes?

3. Do you think that a pig's eyes look intelligent? What color are they? Do you think the pig can see well?

4. Is the pig's head straight in front or is it dished? Is this dished appearance ever found in wild hogs? Do the ears stand out straight or are they lopped? What advantage is the wedge-shaped head to the wild hogs?

5. How is the pig covered? Do you think the hair is thick enough to keep off flies? Why does the pig wallow in the mud? Is it because the animal is dirty by nature or because it is trying to keep clean? Do the hog's bristles stand up if it is angry?

6. If the pig could have its natural food what would it be and where would it be found? Why and on what should pigs be pastured? What do pigs find in the forest to eat? What kind of bacon is considered the best?

7. On how many toes does the pig walk? Are there other toes on which it does not walk? If wading in the mud are the two hind toes of use? Do wild pigs run rapidly? Do tame pigs run rapidly if they are not too fat? Do you think the pig can swim? Do you think that the pig's tail is of any use or merely an ornament?

8. What cries and noises do the pigs make which we can understand?

9. How do hogs fight each other? When the boars fight, how do they attack or ward off the enemy? Where do we get the expression "going sidewise like a hog to war"?

10. How many breeds of pigs do you know? Describe them.

11. What instances have you heard that show the hog's intelligence?

FLOWERLESS PLANTS

Ferns

MANY interesting things about ferns may be taught to the young child, but the more careful study of these plants is better adapted to the pupils in the higher grades, and is one of the wide-open doors that leads directly from nature-study to systematic science. While the pupils are studying the different forms in which ferns bear their fruit, they can make collections of all the ferns of the locality. Since ferns are easily pressed and are beautiful objects when mounted on white paper, the making of a fern herbarium is a delightful pastime; or leaf-prints may be made which give beautiful results; but, better perhaps, than either collections or prints, are pencil or water-color drawings with details of the fruiting organs enlarged. Such a portfolio is not only a thing of beauty but the close observation needed for drawing brings much knowledge to the artist.

References.— *Our Ferns in Their Haunts*, W. N. Clute, (of greatest value to teachers because it gives much of fern literature); *How to Know the Ferns*, Parsons; *Ferns*, Waters; *New England Ferns*, Eastman.

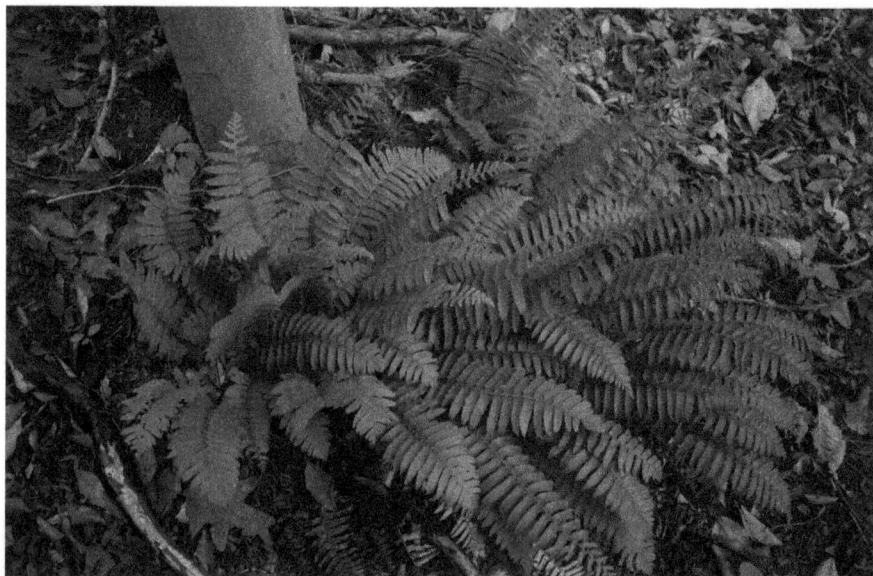

The Christmas Fern

"No shivering frond that shuns the blast sways on its slender chaffy stem;
Full veined and lusty green it stands, of all the wintry woods the gem."
—W. N. Clute.

The rootstock of the fern is an humble example of "rising on step-ping stones of our dead selves," this being almost literally true of the tree-ferns. The rootstock which is a stem and not a root—has, like other stems, a growing tip from which, each year, it sends up into the world several beautiful green fronds, and numerous rootlets down into the earth. These graceful fronds rejoice the world and our eyes for the summer, and make glad the one who, in winter, loves to wander often in the woods to inquire after the welfare of his many friends during their period of sleeping and waking. These fronds, after giving their message of winter cheer, and after the following summer has made the whole woodland green and the young fronds are growing thriftily from the tip of the rootstock, die down, and in midsummer we can find the old fronds lying sere and brown, with broken stipes, just back of the new fern clump; if we examine the rootstock we can detect behind them, remains of the stems of the fronds of year before last; and still farther behind we may trace all the stems of fronds which gladdened the world three years ago. Thus we learn that this rootstock may have been creeping on an inch or so each season for many years, always busy with the present and giving no heed to its dead past. One of the chief differences between our ferns and the tree-ferns of the tropics, which we often see in greenhouses, is that in the tree-fern the rootstock rises in the air instead of creeping on,

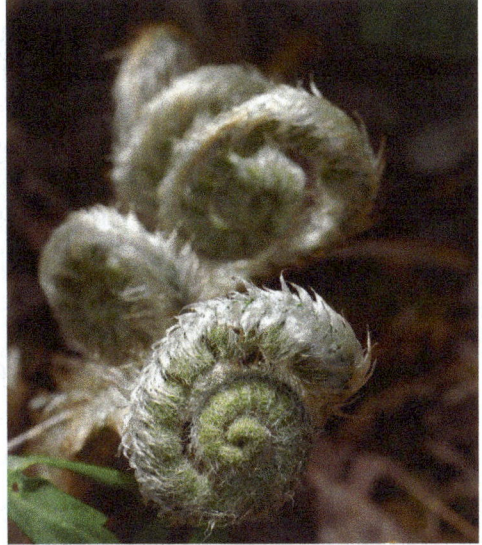

Coiled immature fronds

or below, the surface of the ground. This upright rootstock of the tree-fern also bears fronds at its tip, and its old fronds gradually die down, leaving it rough below its crown of green plumes.

The Christmas fern has its green stipe, or petiole, and its rachis, or midrib, more or less covered with ragged, brownish scales, which give it an unkempt appearance. Its pinnae, or leaflets, are individually very pretty; in color they are dark, shining green, lance-shaped, with a pointed lobe or ear at the base projecting upward. The edges of the pinnae are delicately toothed, each point armed with a little spine, and the veins are fine, straight and free to the margin; the lower pinnae often have the earlike lobe completely severed.

In studying a fertile fern from above, we notice that about a dozen pairs of the pinnae near the tip are narrowed and roughened and are more distinctly toothed on the margins. Examining them underneath, we find on each a double row of circular raised dots which are the fruit-dots, or sori; there is a row between the midrib and margin on each side, and also a double row extending up into the point at the base. Early in the season these spots look like pale blisters, later they turn pale brown, each blister having a depression at its center; by the middle of June, masses of tiny globules, not larger than pin points, push out from beneath the margin of these dots. The blisterlike membrane is simply a cover for the growing spores, and is called the *indusium;* by July it shrivels into an irregular scroll, still clinging to the pinnule by its depressed center; and by this time the profusion of tiny globules covers the entire under side of the pinna like a brown fuzz. If we scrape off some of this fuzz and examine it with a lens, we can see that it consists of numberless little globules, each with a stem to attach it to the leaf; these are the spore-cases, or sporangia, each globule being packed full of spores which, even through the lens, look like yellowish powder. But each particle of this dust has its own structure and contains in its heart the living fern-substance.

Not all the fronds of the fern clump bear these fruit-dots. The ones we select for decoration are usually the sterile fronds, for the fertile ones are not so graceful, and many ignorant people think the brown spore-cases are a fungus. The Christmas fern being evergreen

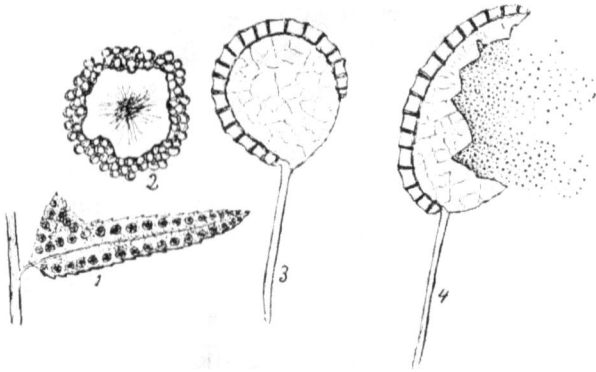

1. Fertile leaflet of Christmas fern showing indusia and spore-cases.
2. An indusium and spore-cases, enlarged. 3. A spore-case, enlarged.
4. A spore-case discharging spores, enlarged.

and very firm in texture, is much used in holiday decoration, hence its common name, which is more easily remembered than *Polystichum acrostichoides,* which is its real name. It loves to grow in well-shaded woodlands, liking better the trees which shed their leaves than the evergreens; it is indeed well-adapted to thrive in damp, cold shade; it is rarely found on slopes which face the south, and sunshine kills it.

LESSON

Leading thought— The fern has a creeping underground stem called the rootstock, which pushes forward and sends up fresh fronds each year. Some of the fronds of the Christmas fern bear spores on the lower surface of the terminal pinnae.

Method— This lesson should be given during the latter part of May, when the fruit-dots are still green. Take up a fern and transplant it, in a dish of moss, in the schoolroom, and later plant it in some convenient shady place. The pupils should sketch the fertile frond from the upper side so as to fix in their minds the contracted pinnae of the tip; one of the lower pinnae should be drawn in detail, showing the serrate edge, the ear and the venation. The teacher should use the following terms constantly and insistently, so as to make the fern nomenclature a part of the school vocabulary, and thus fit the pupils for using fern manuals.

Common polypody, often mistaken for the Christmas fern

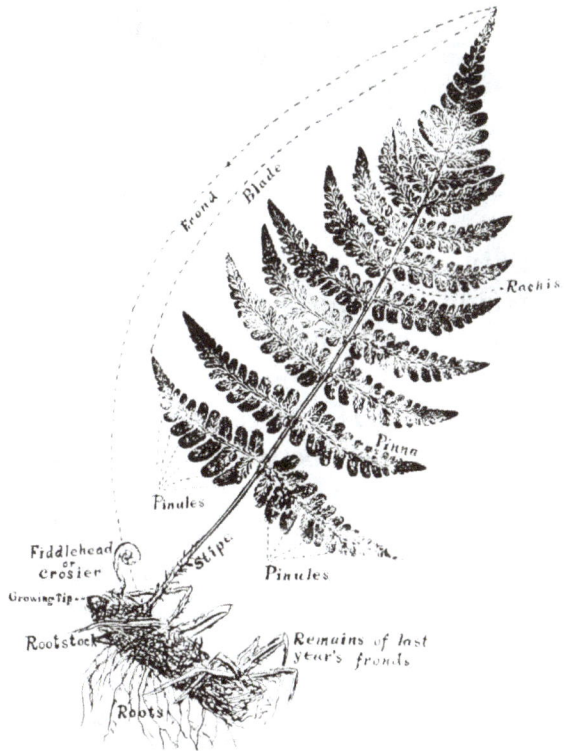

Leaf-print of a fern with the parts named. This fern is twice pinnate.

Newly unfurled frond

A *frond* is all of the fern which grows on one stem from the rootstock; the *blade* is that portion which bears leaflets; the *stipe* is the stem or petiole; the *rachis* is the midrib and is a continuation of the stipe; the *pinnule* is a leaflet of the last division; the *pinna* is a chief division of the midrib or rachis when the fern is compound; the *sori* are the fruit dots; the *indusium* is the membrane covering the fruiting organs; the *sporangia* are the tiny brown globules, and are the spore-cases; the *spores* make up the fine dust which comes from the spore-cases. It would be well to make a diagram on the blackboard of the fern with its parts named, so that the pupils may consult it while studying ferns.

Observations—

1. Study a stump of the Christmas ferns. Are there any withered fronds? Where do they join the rootstock? Do the green fronds come from the same place on the rootstock as the withered ones? Do the green ferns come from near the tip of the rootstock? Can you find the growing tip of the rootstock? Can you trace back and find where the fronds of last year and year before last grew? Does that part of the rootstock seem alive now? Can you find the true root of the fern?

2. Take a frond of the Christmas fern. Is the stem, or stipe, and the midrib, or rachis, smooth or rough? What color are the scales of the stalk? Do you think that these scales once wrapped the fern bud?

3. Does each frond of a clump have the same number of pinnae on each side? Can you find fronds where the pinnae near the tip are narrower than those below? Take a lower pinna and draw it carefully, showing its shape, its edges and its veins. Is there a point, or ear, at

the base of every pinna? Is it a separate lobe or a mere point of the pinna?

4. Take one of the narrow pinnae near the tip of the frond, and examine it beneath. Can you see some circular, roundish blisterlike dots? Are they dented at the center? How many of these dots on a pinna? Make a little sketch showing how they are arranged on the pinna and on the little earlike point. Look at the fruiting pinnae of a fern during July, and describe how they look then.

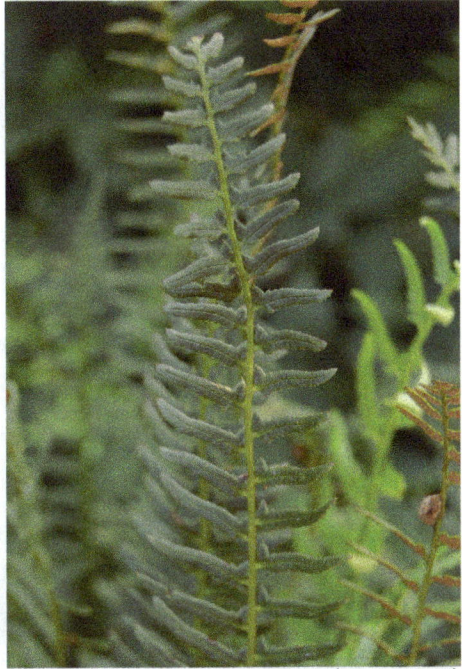

Mature sterile frond

5. Do all the fronds of a fern clump have these narrowed spore-bearing pinnae? Do you know what those fronds are called that bear the fruit-dots?

6. Where do you find the Christmas fern growing? Do you ever find it in a sunny place? Why is it called the Christmas fern?

FERN SONG

Dance to the beat of the rain, little Fern
And spread out your palms again,
And say, "Tho' the sun
Hath my vesture spun,
He had labored, alas, in vain,
But for the shade
That the Cloud hath made,
And the gift of the Dew and the Rain."
Then laugh and upturn
All your fronds, little Fern,
And rejoice in the beat of the rain!

—JOHN B. TABB.

The Bracken

TEACHER'S STORY

It is well for the children to study the animals and plants which have a world-wide distribution. There is something comforting in finding a familiar plant in strange countries; and when I have found the bracken on the coast ranges of California, on the rugged sides of the Alps, and in many other far places, I have always experienced a thrill of delightful memories of the fence corners of the homestead farm. Since the bracken is so widespread, it is natural that it should find a place in literature and popular legend. As it clothes the mountains of Scotland, it is much sung of in Scottish poetry. Many superstitions cluster around it—its seed, if caught at midnight on a white napkin, is supposed to render the possessor invisible. Professor Clute, in Our Ferns in Their Haunts, gives a delightful chapter about the relation of the bracken to people.

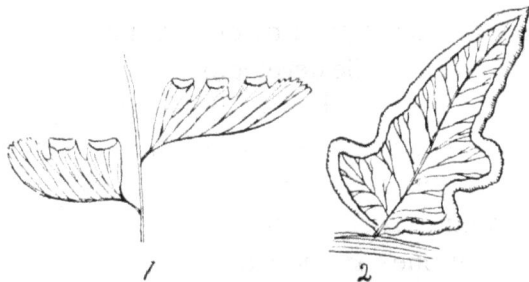

1. Fruiting pinnules of the maiden-hair fern, enlarged. 2. Fruiting pinnule of the bracken, enlarged. In both these species the spores are borne under the recurved edges of the pinnules.

For nature-study purposes, the bracken is valuable as a lesson on the intricate patterns of the fern leaf; it is in fact a lesson in pinnateness. The two lower branches are large and spreading and are in themselves often three times pinnate; the branches higher up are twice pinnate; while the main branch near the tip is once pinnate, and at the tip is merely lobed. The lesson, as illustrated in the diagram of the fern, should be well learned for future study, because this nomenclature is used in all the fern manuals. The fact that a pinnule is merely the last division of a frond, whether it be twice or thrice pinnate, should also be understood.

The bracken does not love complete shade and establishes itself in waste places, living contentedly in not too shaded locations; it is especially fond of woodsides, and fence corners on high and cold land. As Professor Clute says, "It is found both in woodland and in the open field; its favorite haunt is neither, but is that half-way ground where man leaves off and nature begins, the copse or the thicket." With us it usually grows about three feet high, but varies much in this respect. The great triangular fronds often measure two or three feet across, and are supposed to bear a likeness to an eagle with spread wings. Its rootstock is usually too deeply embedded in earth for the study of any except the most energetic; it is about the size of a lead pencil and is black and smooth; in its way it is a great traveler, sending up fronds fifteen or twenty feet from its starting place. It also sends off branching rootstocks.

The fruiting pinnules look as if they were hemmed and the edges of the hems embroidered with brown wool; but the embroidery is simply the spore-cases pushing out from under the folded margin which protected them while developing.

Much on which to base necromancy has been found in the figure shown in the cross-section of the stem or stipe. The letter C, supposed to stand for Christ, thus made is a potent protection from witches. But this figure has also been compared to the devil's hoof, an oak tree, or the initial of one's sweetheart, and all these imaginings have played their part in the lives of the people of past ages. It was believed in England that burning the bracken from the fields brought rain; the roots in time of scarcity have been ground and mixed with flour to make bread. The young ferns, or croziers, are sometimes cooked and eaten like asparagus. The fronds have been used extensively for tanning leather and for packing fish and fruit, and when burned their ashes are used instead of soap.

In Europe, bracken grows so rankly that it is used for roof-thatching and for the bedding of cattle. The name "brake," which is loosely used for all ferns, comes from the word "bracken;" some people think that brakes are different from ferns, whereas this is simply a name which has strayed from the bracken to other species. Its scientific name, *Pteris aquilina*, signifies eagle's wing.

LESSON

Leading thought— The bracken is a fern which has taken possession of the world. It is much branched and divided, and it covers the ground in masses where it grows. The edges of its pinnules are folded under to protect the spores.

Method— Bring to the schoolroom large and small specimens of the bracken, and after a study is made tell about the superstitions connected with this fern and as far as possible interest the pupils in its literature.

Observations—

1. Do you find the bracken growing in the woods or open places? Do you find it in the cultivated fields? How high does it stand? Could you find the rootstock?

2. Take a bracken frond. What is its general shape? Does it remind you of an eagle with spread wings? Look at its very tip. Is it pinnate or

Fronds of the bracken fern

merely lobed? Can you find a place farther down where the leaflets, or pinnules, are not joined at their bases? This is once pinnate. Look farther down and find a pinna that is lobed at the tip; at the base it has distinct pinnules. This is twice pinnate. Look at the lowest divisions of all. Can you find any part of this which is three times pinnate? Four times pinnate? Pinna means feather, pinnate therefore means feathered. If a thing is once pinnate, it means that it has divisions along each side similar to a feather; twice pinnate means that each feather has little feathers along each side; thrice pinnate means that the little feathers have similar feathers along each side, and so on.

3. Can you see if the edges of the pinnules are folded under? Lift up one of these edges and see if you can find what is growing beneath it. How do these folded margins look during August and September?

4. Cut the stem, or stipe, of a bracken across and see the figure in it. Does it look like the initial C? Or a hoof, or an oak tree, or another initial?

5. Discover, if you can, the different uses which people of other countries find for this fern.

How a Fern Bud Unfolds

TEACHER'S STORY

Of all "plant babies," that of the fern is most cozily cuddled; one feels when looking at it, that not only are its eyes shut but its fists are tightly closed. But the first glance at one of these little woolly spirals gives us but small conception of its marvelous enfolding, all so systematic and perfect that it seems another evidence of the divine origin of mathematics. Every part of the frond is present in that bud, even to the fruiting organs; all the pinny and the pinnules are packed in the smallest compass—each division, even to the smallest pinnule, coiled in a spiral towards its base. These coiled fern buds are called crosiers; they are woolly, with scales instead of hairs, and are thus well blanketed. Some botanists object to the comparison of the woolly or fuzzy clothing of young plants with the blankets of human infants. It is true that the young plant is not kept at a higher temperature by this covering; but because of it, transpiration which is a cooling process is prevented, and thus the plant is kept warmer. When the fern commences to grow, it stretches up and seems to lean over backward in its effort to be bigger. First the main stem, or rachis, loosens its coil; but before this is completed, the pinnae, which are coiled at right angles to the main stem, begin to unfold; a little later the pinnules, which are folded at right angles to the pinnae, loosen and seem to stretch and yawn before taking a look at the world which they have just entered; it may be several days before all signs of the complex coiling disappear. The crosiers of the bracken are queer looking creatures, soon developing three claws which some people say look like the talons of an eagle; and so intricate is the action of their multitudinous spirals, that to watch them unfolding impresses one as in the presence of a miracle.

LESSON

Leading thought— All of the parts of the frond of a fern are tightly folded spirally within the bud, and every lobe of every leaflet is also folded in a spiral.

Method— The bracken crosier is a most illuminating object for this lesson, because it has so many divisions and is so large; it is also convenient, because it may be found in September. However, any fern bud will do. The lesson may be best given in May when the woodland ferns are starting. A fern root with its buds should be brought to the schoolroom, where the process of unfolding may be watched at leisure.

Observations—

1. Take a very young bud. How does it look? Do you see any reason why ignorant people call these buds caterpillars? Can you see why they are popularly called "fiddle heads"? What is their true name? How many turns of the coil can you count? What is the covering of the crosier? Do you think this cover is a protection? How is the stem grooved to make the spiral compact?

2. Take a crosier a little further advanced. How are its pinnae folded? How is each pinnule of each pinna folded? How is each lobe of a pinnule folded? Is each smaller part coiled toward each larger part?

3. Write in your note-book the story of the unfolding fern, and sketch its stages each day from the time it is cuddled down in a spiral until it is a fully expanded frond.

The Fruiting of the Fern

"If we were required to know the position of the fruit-dots or the character of the indusium, nothing could be easier than to ascertain it; but if it is required that you be affected by ferns, that they amount to anything, signify anything to you, that they be another sacred scripture and revelation to you, help to redeem your life, this end is not so easily accomplished."

—THOREAU.

THE fern, like the butterfly, seems to have several this-world incarnations; and perhaps the most wonderful of these is the spore. Shake the dust out of the ripened fern and each particle, although too small for the naked eye to see, has within it the possibilities of developing a mass of graceful ferns. Each spore has an outside hard layer, and within this an atom of fern-substance; but it cannot be developed unless it falls into some warm, damp place favorable for

158

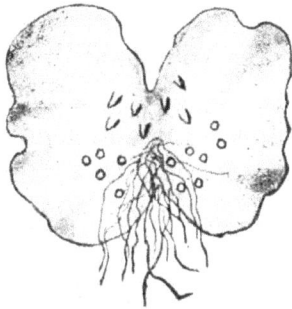

Prothallium, greatly enlarged, showing the two kinds of pockets and the rootlets

its growth; it may have to wait many years before chance gives it this favorable condition, but it is strong and patient and retains its vital power for years. There are cases known where spores grew after twenty years of waiting. But what does this microscopic atom grow into? It develops into a tiny heart-shaped, leaflike structure which botanists call the prothallium; this has on its lower side little roots which reach down into the soil for nourishment; and on its upper surface are two kinds of pockets, one round and the other long. In the round pockets are developed bodies which may be compared to the pollen; and in the long pockets, bodies which may be compared to the ovules of flowering plants. In the case of ferns, water is necessary to float the pollen from the round pockets to the ovules in the long pockets. From a germ thus fertilized in one of the long pockets, a little green fern starts to grow, although it may be several years before it becomes a plant strong enough to send up fronds with spore-dots on them.

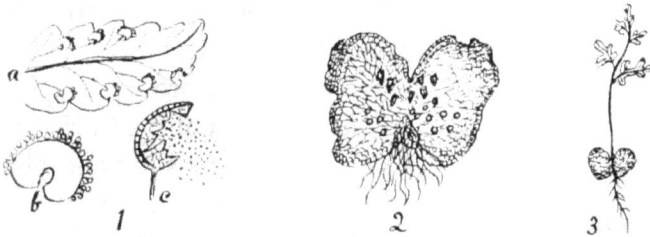

The life of a fern.
1. a, pinna bearing fruit; b, a fruit-dot, enlarged, showing spore-cases pushing out around the edges of the indusium; c, spore-case, enlarged, showing how it discharges the spores. 2. Prothallium, enlarged. 3. Young fern growing from the prothallium.

To study the structure of the spore requires the highest powers of the microscope; and even the prothallium in most species is very small, varying from the size of a pin-head to that of a small pea, and it is therefore quite difficult to find. I found some once on a mossy log that bridged a stream, and I was never so triumphant over any other outdoor achievement. They may be found in damp places, in greenhouses, but the teacher will be very fortunate who is able to show her pupils this stage of the fern. The prothallium is a stage

1. Fruiting pinnule of the boulder fern, enlarged.
2. Fruiting pinnules of spleenwort, enlarged.

Fruiting pinnules of ever-green wood fern.

of the fern to be compared to the flower and seed combined in the higher plants; but this is difficult for young minds to comprehend. I like to tell the children that the fern, like a butterfly, has several stages: Beginning with the spore-bearing fern, we next have the spores, next the prothallium stage, and then the young fern. While in the other case we have first the egg, then the caterpillar, then the chrysalis, and then the butterfly. Looking at the ripe fruit-dots on the lower side of the fern leaf, we can easily see with a lens a mass of tiny globules; each one of these is a spore-case, or sporangium (plural *sporangia*), and is fastened to the leaf by a stalk and has, almost encircling it, a jointed ring.

When the spores are ripe, this ring straightens out and ruptures the globule, and out fly the spores. By scraping a little of the brown fuzz from a fruiting pinna of the Christmas fern upon a glass slide and placing a cover glass upon it, we find it very easy to examine through the microscope, and we are able thus to find the spore-cases in all stages, and to see the spores distinctly. The spore-cases may also be seen with a hand lens, the spores seeming then to be mere dust.

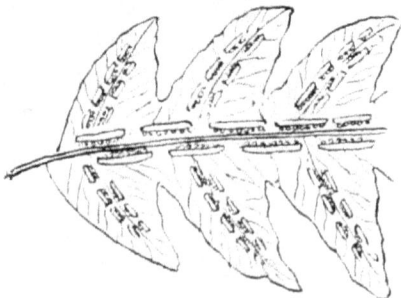

Fruiting pinnules of the chain fern.

The different ways the ferns blanket their spore-cases is a delightful study, and one which the pupils enjoy very much. All of our common ferns except the careless little polypody thus protect their spores.

160

A sensitive fern, showing sterile and fertile fronds.

Whether this blanket be circular, or horseshoe-shaped, or oblong, or in the form of pocket or cup, depends upon the genus to which the fern belongs. The little protecting blanket-membrane is called the *indusium*, and while its shape distinguishes the genus, the position in which it grows determines the species. I shall never forget my surprise and delight when, as a young girl, I visited the Philadelphia Centennial Exposition, and there in the great conservatories saw for the first time the tree-ferns of the tropics. One of these was labelled *Dicksonia*, and mystified, I asked the privilege of examining the fronds for fruiting organs. When lo! the indusium proved to be a little cup, borne at the base of the tooth of the pinnule, exactly like that of our boulder fern, which is also a Dicksonia. I had a sudden feeling that I must have fern friends all over the world.

The children are always interested in the way the maidenhair folds over the tips of her scallops to protect her spore nursery; and while many of our ferns have their fertile fronds very similar in form to the sterile ones, yet there are many common ferns with fertile fronds that look so different from the others, that one would not think they were originally of the same pattern; but although their pinnules are

Diagram of he interrupted fern, showing the three pairs of fruiting pinnae, and a part of one of these enlarged. This fern often has fronds four or five feet high

changed into cups, or spore-pockets, of various shapes, if they be examined carefully they will be seen to have the same general structure and the same divisions however much contracted, as have the large sterile fronds. The Osmundas, which include the interrupted, the cinnamon and the flowering ferns, are especially good for this part of the lesson. The sensitive fern, so common in damp places in open fields, is also an excellent illustration of this method of fruiting. While studying the ferns, the teacher should lay stress upon the fact that they represent the earliest and simplest forms of plants, that they reached the zenith of their growth in the Carboniferous age, and that, to a large extent, our coal is composed of them. It is interesting to think that the exquisite and intricate leaf patterns of the ferns should belong to a primitive type. Often when I have watched the forming by the frost, of the exquisite fernlike pictures on the windowpane, I have wondered if, after all, the first expression of the Creator did not find form in the most exquisite grace and beauty; and if perchance the first fishes, so fierce and terrible, did not mark the introduction of Satan.

LESSON

Leading thought— Ferns do not have flowers, but they produce spores. Spores are not seeds; but they grow into something which may be compared to a true seed, and this in turn develops into young ferns. Each genus of ferns has its own peculiar way of protecting its spores; and if we learn these different ways, we can recognize ferns without effort.

Method— July is the best time for this lesson, which is well adapted for summer schools or camping trips. However, if it is desired to use it

as a school lesson, it should be begun in June, when the fruiting organs are green, and it may be finished in September after the spores are discharged. Begin with the Christmas fern, which ripens in June, and make the fruiting of this species a basis for comparison. Follow this with other wood ferns which bear fruit-dots on the back of the fronds. Then study the ferns which live in more open places, and which have fronds changed in form to bear the spores—like the sensitive, the ostrich, the royal and the flowering ferns. A study of the interrupted fern is a desirable preparation for the further study of those which have special fruiting fronds; the interrupted fern has, at about the middle of its frond, three pinnae on each side, fitted for spore-bearing, the pinnules being changed into globular cups filled with spore-cases.

While not absolutely necessary, it is highly desirable that each member of the class should look at a fruit-dot of some fern through a three-quarters objective of a compound microscope, and then examine the spore-cases and the spores through a one-sixth objective.

It must be remembered that this lesson is for advanced grades, and is a preparation for systematic scientific work. If a microscope is not available, the work may be done with a hand lens aided by pictures.

Observations—

1. Take a fern that is in fruit; lay it on a sheet of white paper and leave it thus for a day or two, where it will not be disturbed and where there is no draught; then take it up carefully; the form of the fern will be outlined in dust. What is this dust?

2. What conditions must the spores have in order to grow? What do they grow into? (See First Studies of Plant Life by Atkinson, p. 207).

3. Look at a ripe fruit-dot on the back of a fern leaf and see where the spores come from. Can you see with a lens many little, brown globules? Can you see that some of them are torn open? These are the spore-cases, called *sporangia,* each globule being packed with spores. Can you see how the sporangia are fastened to the leaf by little stems?

4. Almost all our common wood ferns have the spore-cases protected by a thin membrane, the spore-blanket, when very young; this little membrane is called the *indusium,* and it is of different shape in those ferns which do not have the same surname, or generic name. Study as many kinds of wood ferns as you can find. If the blanket, or indusium, is circular with a dent at the center where it is fastened to the leaf, and the spore-cases push out around the margin, it is a *Christmas fern;* if horseshoe-shaped, it is one of the *wood ferns;* if oblong, in rows on each side of the midrib, it is a *chain fern;* but if oblong and at an angle to the midrib, it is a *spleenwort;* if it is pocket-shaped and opening at one side, it is a *bladder fern;* if it is cup-shaped, it is a *boulder fern;* if it breaks open and lays back in star shape, it is a *woodsia;* if the edge of the fern leaf is folded over all along its margin to protect the spore-cases, it is a *bracken;* if the tips of the scallops of the leaf be delicately folded over to make a spore blanket, it is the *maidenhair.*

5. If you know of swampy land where there are many tall brakes, look for a kind that has some of its pinnae withered and brown. Examine these withered pinnae, and you will see that they are not withered at all but are changed into little cups to hold spore-cases. This is the *interrupted fern.* The *flowering fern* has the pinnae at its tip changed into cups for spore-cases. The *cinnamon fern,* which grows in swampy

places, has whole fronds which are cinnamon-colored and look withered, but which bear the spores. The *ostrich fern*, which has fronds which look like magnificent ostrich feathers, has stiff, little stalks of fruiting fronds very unlike the magnificent sterile fronds. The *sensitive fern*, which grows in damp meadows and along roadsides, also has contracted fruiting fronds. If you find any of these, compare carefully the fruiting with the sterile fronds, and note in each case the resemblance in branching and in pinnules and also the shape of the openings through which the spores are sifted out.

6. Gather and press specimens of as many ferns in the fruiting stage as you can find, taking both sterile and fruiting fronds in those species which have this specialization.

7. Read in the geologies about the ferns which helped to make our coal beds.

Supplementary reading. — *The Story of a Fern*; *First Studies of Plant Life*, Atkinson; *The Petrified Fern*, M. L. B. Branch.

"*Nature made ferns for pure leaves to see what she could do in that line.*"
—THOREAU.

165

The Field Horsetail

These queer, pale plants grow in sandy or gravelly soil, and since they appear so early in the spring they are objects of curiosity to children. The stalk is pale and uncanny looking; the pinkish stem, all the same size from bottom to top, is ornamented at intervals with upward-pointing, slender, black, sharp-pointed scales, which unite at the bottom and encircle the stalk in a slightly bulging ring, a ring which shows a ridge for every scale, extending down the stem. These black scales are really leaves springing from a joint in the stem, but they forgot long ago how to do a leaf's work of getting food from the air. The "blossom" which is not a real blossom in the eye of the botanist, is made up of rows of tiny discs which are set like miniature toadstools around the central stalk. Before it is ripe, there extends back from the edge of each disc a row of little sacs stuffed so full of green spores that they look united like a row of tiny green ridges. The discs at the top of the fertile spike discharge their spores first, as can be seen by shaking the plant over white paper, the falling spores looking like pale green pow-

166

der. The burst and empty sacs are whitish, and hang around the discs in torn scallops, after the spores are shed. The spores, when seen under the microscope, are wonderful objects, each a little green ball with four spiral bands wound about it. These spirals uncoil and throw the spore, giving it a movement as of something alive. The motor power in these living springs is the absorbing of moisture.

The beginning of the sterile shoot can be seen like a green bit of the blossom spike of the plantain; but later, after the fertile stalks have died down, these cover the ground with their strange fringes.

The person who first called these sterile plants "horsetails" had an overworked imagination, or none at all; for the only quality the two

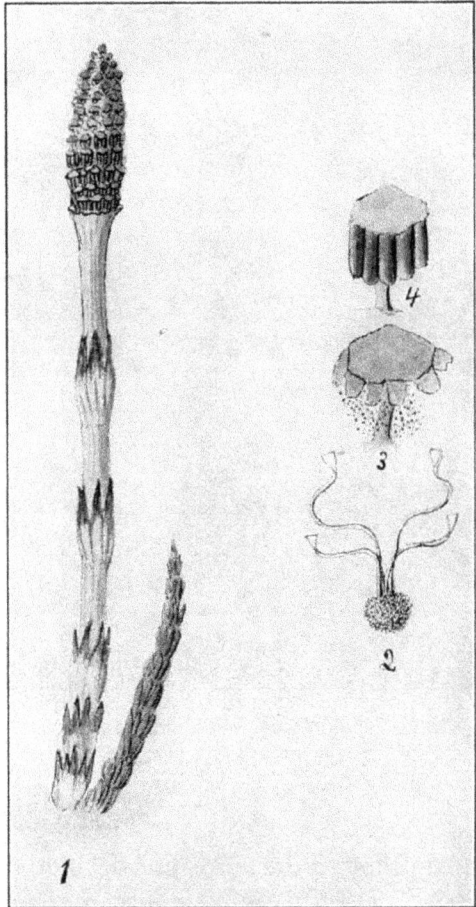

1, Fertile plant of the field horsetail; 2, spore; 3, disk discharging spores; 4, disk with spore-sacs.

have in common is brushiness. A horse which had the hair of its tail set in whorls with the same precision as this plant has its branches would be one of the world's wonders. The *Equicetum* is one of the plants which give evidence of nature's resourcefulness; its remote ancestors probably had a whorl of leaves at each joint or node of the main stem and branches; but the plant now having so many green branches, does not really need the leaves, and thus they have been reduced to mere points, and look like nothing but "trimming," they are so purely ornamental. Each little cup or socket, of the joint or node, in branch or stem, has a row of points around its margin, and these points are

Lycopodiella alopecuroides. *This plant is common in the bogs of pine-barrens.*

terminals of the angles in the branch. If a branch is triangular in cross section, it will have three points at its socket, if quadrangular it will have four points, and the main stem may have six or a dozen, or even more points. The main stem and branches are made up entirely of these segments, each set at its lower end in the socket of the segment behind or below it. These green branches, rich in chlorophyl, manufacture for the plant all the food that it needs. Late in the season this food is stored in the rootstocks, so that early next spring the fertile plants, nourished by this stored material, are able to push forth before most other plants, and thus develop their spores early in the season. There is a prothallium stage as in the ferns.

Above where the whorl of stems comes from the main branch, may be seen a row of upward-standing points which are the remnants of leaves; each branch as it leaves the stem is set in a little dark cup with a toothed rim. There is a nice gradation from the stout lower part of the stem to the tip, which is as delicate as one of the side branches.

The rootstock dies out behind the plant and pushes on ahead like the rootstock of ferns. The true roots may be seen attached on the under side. The food made in the summer is stored in little tubers, which may be seen in the rootstocks.

LESSON

THE FERILE PLANTS

Leading thought— The horsetail is a plant that develops spores instead of seeds, and has green stems instead of leaves.

Method— In April and May, when the children are looking for flowers, they will find some of these weird looking plants. These should be brought to the schoolroom and the observation lesson given there.

Observations—

1. Where are these plants found? On what kind of soil?

2. In what respect does this plant differ from other plants in appearance? Can you find any green part to it?

3. What color is the stem?

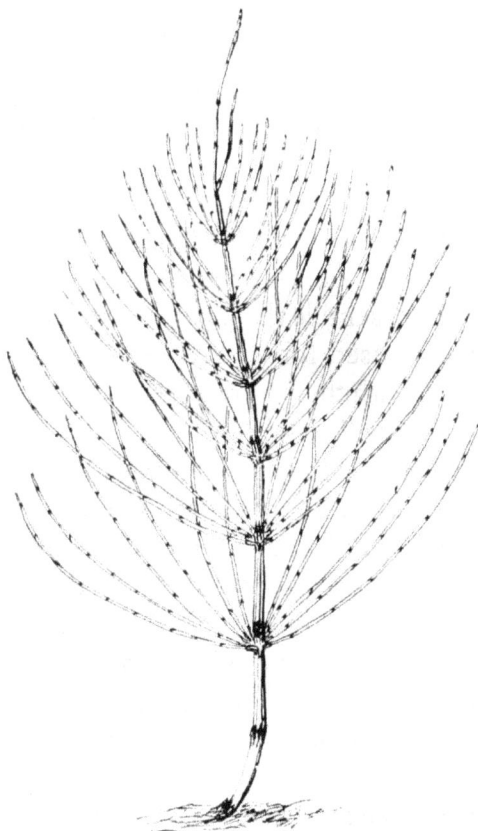

The sterile plant of the field horsetail, one-half natural size.

Is it the same size its whole length? Is it smooth or rough?

4. Do you see any leaves on the stems? Do you see the black-pointed scales? In which direction do these scales point? Are they united at the bottom? What sort of a ring do they make around the stem? Split a stem lengthwise and see if there are joints, or nodes, where the ring joins the stalk.

5. How does the "blossom" look? What color are the little discs that make up the blossom? How are the discs set?

6. Take one of the plants which has the discs surrounded by green ridges. Shake it over a white paper. What comes from it? Where does it come from? Which discs on the stalk shed the green spores first?

THE STERILE PLANTS

Leading thought— The horsetail or *Equicetum* is nourished by very different looking stems than those which bore the spores. It lacks leaves, but its branches are green and do the work of making food for the plant.

Method— The sterile plants of the horsetail do not appear for several weeks after the fertile ones; they are much more numerous, and do not resemble the fertile plants in form or color. These sterile plants may be used for a lesson in September or October. Some of these plants with their roots may be brought into the schoolroom for study.

Observations—

1. Has this plant any leaves? How does it make and digest its food without leaves? What part of it is green? Wherever there is green in a plant, there is the chlorophyl-factory for making food. In the horsetail, then, what part of the plant does the work of leaves?

2. Take off one little branch and study with the lens. How does it look? Pull it apart. Where does it break easily? How many joints, or nodes, are there in the branch?

3. Study the socket from which one of the segments was pulled off. What do you see around its edge? How many of these points? Look at the branch in cross section. How many angles has it? What relation do the points bear to the angles? Do you think these points are all there are left of true leaves?

4. How do the little green branches come off the main stem? How many in a place? How many whorls of branches on the main stem?

5. Study the bases of the branches. What do you see? Look directly above where the whorl of branches comes off the main stem. What do you see? Cut the main stem in cross-section just below this place, and see if there are as many little points as there are angles, or ridges, in the stem. Do you suppose these little points are the remnants of leaves on the main stem?

6. What kind of root has the horsetail? Do you think this long running root is the true root or an underground stem? Where are the true roots? Do you think the rootstock dies off at the oldest end each year, like the fern? Can you find the little tubers in the rootstock, which contain nourishment for next year's spore-bearing stalks?

Haircap moss

The Hair-Cap Moss, or Pigeon Wheat

TEACHER'S STORY

The mosses are a special delight to children because they are green and beautiful before other plants have gained their greenness in the spring and after they have lost it in the fall; to the discerning eye, a mossy bank or a mossy log is a thing of beauty always. When we were children we regarded moss as a forest for fairy folk, each moss stem being a tree, and we naturally concluded that fairy forests were ever-green. We also had other diversions with pigeon wheat, for we took the fruiting stem, pulled the cap off the spore-capsule, tucked the other end of the red stem into the middle of the capsule, making a beautiful coral ring with an emerald "set." To be sure these rings were rather too delicate to last long, but there were plenty more to be had for nothing; so we made these rings into long chains which we wore as necklaces for brief and happy moments, their evanescence being one of their charms.

Pigeon wheat is a rather large moss which grows on dry knolls, usually near the margins of damp woodlands in just those places where wintergreens love to grow. In fall or winter it forms a greenish brown mass of bristling stems; in the early summer the stems are tipped with the vivid green of the new growth. The bristling appearance comes from the long sharp leaves set thickly upon the ruddy brown stems; each leaf is pretty to look at with a lens, which reveals it as thick though narrow, grooved along the middle, the edges usually armed with sharp teeth and the base clasping the stem. These leaves, although so small, are wonderfully made; during the hot, dry weather they shut up lengthwise and twist into the merest threads, in order to keep their soft, green surfaces from losing their moisture by exposure to the air; more than this, they lift themselves and huddle close to the stem, and are thus as snug and safe as may be from the effect of drought; but as soon as the rains come, they straighten back at right angles to the stem, and curve their tips downward in a joyful expanding. Bring in some of this moss and let it dry, and then drop it into a glass of water and watch this miracle of leaf movement! And yet it is no miracle but a mechanism quite automatic—and therefore—like other miracles, when once they are understood.

In early June the mossy knoll shows us the origin of the name pigeon grass or pigeon wheat, for it is then covered with a forest of shining, ruddy, stiff, little stems, each stem bearing on its tip a woolly object about the size of a grain of wheat. But it is safe to say that the pigeons and other birds enjoy our own kind of wheat better than this, which is attributed to them.

A study of one of these wheat grains reveals it as covered with a yellowish, mohair cap, ending in a golden brown peak at its tip, as if it were the original pattern of the toboggan cap; it closes loosely and downily around the stem below. This grain is the spore-capsule of the moss; the hairy cap pulls off easily when seized by its tip. This cap is present at the very beginning, even before the stem lengthens, to protect the delicate tissues of the growing spore-case; it is only through a lens that we can see it in all its silky softness. The capsule revealed by the removal of the cap is a beautiful green object, usually four-sided, set upon an elegant little pedestal where it joins the coral stem, and with a lid on its top like a sugar-bowl cover, with a point instead of a

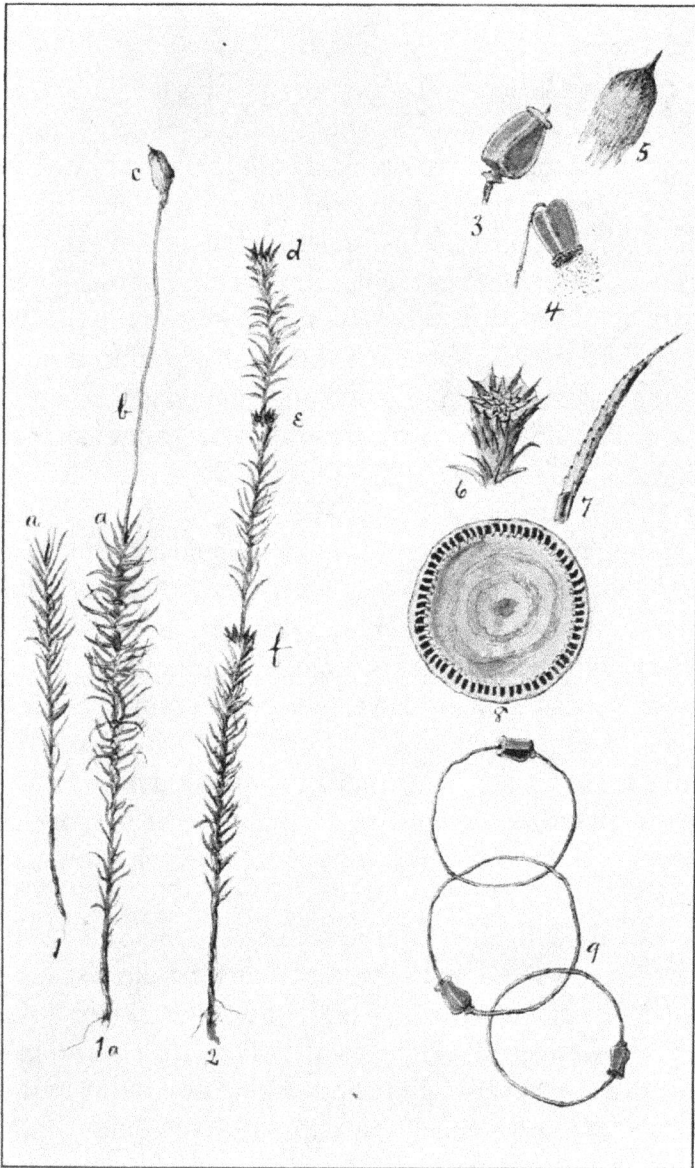

Hair-cap moss.

1, fruit-bearing moss stem before fertilization; 1a, the same stem after fruit is developed; a, where the ovule was before fertilization; b, fruit stem; c, spore-capsule with cap or veil upon it. 2, stem showing the starlike cups; d, the cup in which was developed the pollen which fertilized the ovule at a, this year; e, last year's cup; f, the cup of year before last; only the leaves from e to d are alive. 3, spore capsule with the cap removed, showing the lid. 5, the cap or veil removed. 4, spore capsule with lid off and shaking out the spores. 6, starlike cup in which the pollen is developed. 7, leaf of moss. 8, the top of the spore capsule showing the teeth around the edge between which the spores sift out. 9, a part of a necklace chain made of the spore capsules and their stems.

knob at its center. When the spores are ripe, this lid falls off, and then if we have a lens we may see another instance of moss mechanism. Looking at the uncovered end of the capsule, we see a row of tiny teeth around the margin, which seem to hold down an inner cover with a little raised rim. The botanists have counted these teeth and find there are 64. The teeth themselves are not important, but the openings between them are, since only through these openings can the spores escape. In fact, the capsule is a pepper-box with a grating around its upper edge instead of holes in its cover; and when it is fully ripe, instead of standing right side up, it tips over so as to shake out its spores more easily. These teeth are like the moss leaves; they swell with moisture, and thus in rainy weather they, with the inner cover, swell so that not a single spore can be shaken out. If spores should come out during the rain, they would fall among the parent plants where there is no room for growth. But when they emerge in dry weather, the wind scatters them far and wide where there is room for development.

When seen with the naked eye, the spores seem to be simply fine dust, but each dust grain is able to produce moss plants. However, the spore does not grow up into a plant like a seed, it grows into fine, green, branching threads which push along the surface of damp soil; on these threads little buds appear, each of which grows up into a moss stem.

The spore-capsule is hardly the fruit of the moss plant. If we examine the moss, we find that some stems end in yellowish cups which look almost like blossoms; on closer examination, we find that there are several of these cups, one below the other, with the stem extending up through the middle. The upper cup matured this year, the one below it last year, and so on. These cups are star-pointed, and inside, at the bottom, is a starlike cluster of leaves. Among the leaves of this star-rosette are borne the moss anthers called *antheridii*, too small for us to see without a high power microscope. The pollen from these anthers is blown over to other plants, some of which produce ovules at their very tips, although the ovule has no leaf-rosette to show where it is. This ovule, after receiving the pollen, grows into the spore-capsule supported on its coral stem. These—stem, capsule and all—grow up out of the mother plant, the red stem is enlarged at its base, and fits into the moss stem like a flagstaff in the socket. After the star-shaped cup has shed its pollen, the stem grows up from its center for an inch or so in height and bears new leaves, and next year will bear another starry cup.

The brown leaves on the lower part of the moss stem are dead, and only the green leaves on the upper part are living.

And this is the story of the moss cycle:

1. A plant with an ovule at its tip; another plant with a star-cup holding the moss pollen which is sifted by wind over to the waiting egg.

Common haircap

Close-up of capsules (after shedding of calyptra)

2. The egg or ovule as soon as fertilized develops into a spore-capsule, and is lifted up into the world on a beautiful shining stem and is protected by a silky cap.

3. The cap comes off; the lid of the spore-case falls off, the spores are shaken out and scattered by the wind.

4. Those spores that find fitting places grow into a net of green threads.

5. These green threads send up moss stems which repeat the story.

LESSON

Leading thought— The mosses, like the butterfly and the fern, have several stages in their development. The butterfly stages are the egg, the caterpillar, the chrysalis, the butterfly. The moss stages are the egg (or ovule), the spores, the branching green threads, the moss plants with their green foliage. In June we can easily find all these stages, except perhaps the branching thread stage.

Method— The children should bring to the schoolroom a basin of moss in its fruiting stage; or still better, go with them to a knoll covered with moss. Incidentally tell them that this moss, when dried, is used by the Laplanders for stuffing their pillows, and that the bears use it for their beds. Once, a long time ago, people believed that a plant, by the shape of its leaf or flower, indicated its nature as a medicine, and as this moss looked like hair, the water in which it was steeped was used as a hair tonic.

Observations—

1. Take a moss stem with a grain of pigeon wheat at the end. Examine the lower part of the stalk. How are the leaves arranged on it? Examine one of the little leaves through a lens and describe its shape, its edges, and the way it joins the stem. Are the lower leaves the same color as the upper ones? Why?

2. Describe the pretty shining stem of the fruit, which is called the pedicel. Is it the same color for its entire length? Can you pull it easily from the main plant? Describe how its base is embedded in the tip of the plant.

3. Note the silken cap on a grain of the pigeon wheat. This is called the veil. Is it all the same color? Is it grown fast to the plant at its lower margin? Take it by the tip, and pull it off. Is this done easily? Describe what it covers. This elegant little green vase is called a spore-capsule. How many sides has it? Describe its base which stands upon the stem. Describe the little lid. Pull off the lid; is there another lid below it? Can you see the tiny teeth around the edge which hold this lid in place? Ask your teacher, or read in the books, the purpose of this.

4. Do all the spore vases stand straight up, or do some bend over?

5. Do you think the silken cap falls off of itself after a while? Can you find any capsules where the cap or veil and the lid have fallen off?

See if you can shake any dust out of such a spore vase. What do you think this dust is? Ask your teacher, or read in the books, about moss spores and what happens if they find a damp place in which to grow.

6. Hunt among the moss for some stems that have pretty, yellowish, starlike cups at their tips. How does the inside of one of these cups look? Ask the teacher to tell you what grows in this cup. Look down the stem and see if you can find last year's cup. The cup of two years ago? Measured by these cups how old do you think this moss stem is?

7. Select some stems of moss, both those that bear the fruit and those that bear the cups. After they are dried describe how the leaves look. Examine the plant with a lens and note how these leaves are folded and twisted. Do the leaves stand out from the stem or lie close to it? Is this action of the leaves of any use to the plant in keeping the water from evaporating? How do the star-cups look when dry?

FABELFROH (CC BY-SA 3.0)
Bog haircap moss

FABELFROH (CC BY-SA 3.0)
Bog haircap moss

8. Place these dried stems in a glass of water and describe what happens to the cup. Examine some of the dried moss and the wet moss with a lens, and describe the difference. Of what use to the moss is this power of changing form when damp?

Reference— First Lessons in Plant Life, Atkinson.

Mushrooms and Other Fungi

HERE is something uncanny about plants which have no green parts; they seem like people without blood. It is, therefore, no wonder that many superstitions cluster about toadstools. In times of old, not only did the toads sit on them, but fairies danced upon them and used them for umbrellas. The poisonous qualities of some species made them also a natural ingredient of the witch's cauldron. But science, in these days, brings revelations concerning these mysterious plants which are far more wonderful than the web which superstition wove about them in days of yore.

When we find plants with no green parts which grow and thrive, though unable to manufacture their own organic food through the alchemy of chlorophyl, sunlight and air, we may safely infer that in one way or another they gain the products of this alchemy at second hand. Such plants are either parasites or saprophytes; if parasites, they steal the food from the cells of living plants; if saprophytes, they live on

178

such of this food material as remains in dead wood, withered leaves, or soils enriched by their remains.

Thus, we find mushrooms and other fungus fruiting bodies, pallid, brown-olive, yellow or red in color, but with no signs of the living green of other plants; and this fact re-

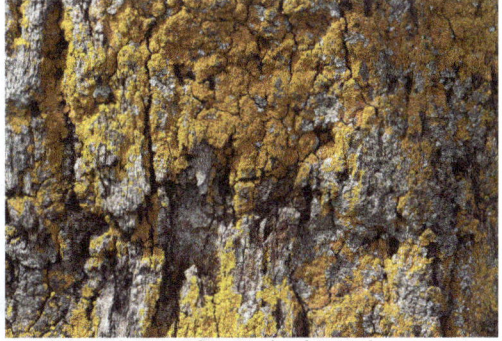

Lichen on the trunk of an oak tree

veals their history. Some of them are parasites, as certain species of bracket fungi which are the deadly enemies of living trees; but most of the fungus species that we ordinarily see are saprophytes, and live on dead vegetation. Fungi, as a whole, are a great boon to the world. Without them our forests would be choked out with dead wood. Decay is simply the process by which fungi and other organisms break down dead material, so that the major part of it returns to the air in gaseous form, and the remainder, now mostly humus, mingles with the soil.

As a table delicacy, mushrooms are highly prized. A very large number of species are edible. But every year the newspapers report deaths resulting from eating the poisonous kinds—the price of an ignorance which comes from a lack of the powers of observation developed in nature-study. It would be very unwise for any teacher to give rules to guide her pupils in separating edible from poisonous mushrooms, since the most careful directions may be disregarded or misunderstood. She should emphasize the danger incurred by mistaking a poisonous for an edible species. One small button of the deadly kind, if eaten, may cause death. A few warning rules may be given, which if firmly impressed on the pupils, may result in saving human life.

First and most important, avoid all mushrooms that are covered with scales, or that have the base of the stem included in a sac, for two of the poisonous species, often mistaken for the common edible mushroom, have these distinguishing characters. Care should be taken that every specimen be collected in a way to show the base of the stem, since in some poisonous species this sac is hidden beneath the soil.

Behind the cap of a mushroom hide the gills

Second, avoid the young, or button, stages, since they are similar in appearance in species that are edible and in those that are poisonous.

Third, avoid those that have milky juices; unless the juices are reddish in color, the mushrooms should not be eaten.

Fourth, avoid those with shiny, thin, or brightly colored caps, and those with whitish or clay-colored spores.

Fifth, no mushroom or puffball should be eaten after its meat has begun to turn brown or has become infested with fly larvae.

How Mushrooms Look and How They Live

THERE are many kinds of mushrooms varying greatly in form, color and size, but wherever they appear it means that sometime previous the mushroom spores have been planted there. There they threw out threads which have penetrated the food substance and gained a successful growth, which finally resulted in sending up into the world the fruiting organs. In general shape these consist of a stem with a cap upon it, making it usually somewhat umbrella-shaped. Attached

180

The deadly amanita, Amanita phalloides.

to the cap, and usually under it, are plate-like growths called gills, or a fleshy surface which is full of pores. In the case of the gills, each side of each plate develops spores. These, as fine as dust, are capable of producing other mushrooms.

In the common edible species of mushroom (*Agaricus campestris*), the stem is white and almost cylindrical, tapering slightly toward the base; it is solid although the core is not so firm as the outside. When it first pushes above the ground, it is in what is called the "button stage" and consists of a little, rounded cap covered with a membrane which is attached to the stem. Later the cap spreads wide, for it is naturally umbrella-shaped, and it tears loose this membrane, leaving a piece of it attached to the stem; this remnant is called the ring or collar. The collar is very noticeable in many species, but in the common mushroom it soon shrivels and disappears. The cap is at first rounded and then convex; its surface is at first smooth, looking soft and silky; but

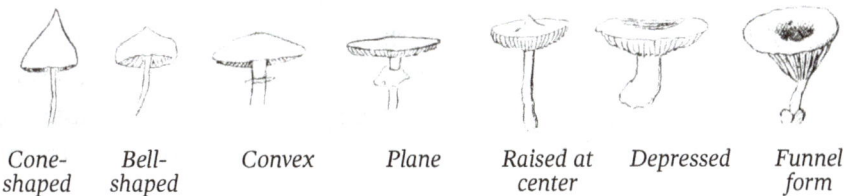

| Cone-shaped | Bell-shaped | Convex | Plane | Raised at center | Depressed | Funnel form |

Mycelium as seen under a log

as the plant becomes old, it is often broken up into triangular scales which are often dark brown; although the color of the cap is usually white or pale brown. The gills beneath the cap are at first white, but later, as the spores mature, they become brownish black because of the ripened spores.

References— *Mushrooms*, a most excellent and practical book with many beautiful pictures, written and illustrated by Professor George F. Atkinson; Henry Holt & Co., N. Y.; *The Mushroom Book*, Marshall, fully illustrated, Doubleday, Page & Co.; *One Thousand American Fungi*, McIlvaine, illustrated, Bowen-Merrill Co.; *Our Edible Toadstools and Mushrooms*, W. H. Gibson, very fully illustrated, Harper and Bros.

Inky cap mushroom

LESSON

Leading thought— Mushrooms are the fruiting organs of the fungi which grow in the form of threads, spreading in every direction through the food material. The dust which falls from ripe mushrooms is made up of spores which are not true seeds, but which will start a new growth of the fungus.

Method—The ideal method would be to study the mushrooms in the field and forest, making an excursion for the purpose of collecting as many species as possible. But the lesson may be given from specimens brought into the schoolroom by pupils, care being taken to bring with them the soil, dead wood or leaves on which they were found growing. After studying one species thus, encourage the pupils to bring in as many others as possible. There are a few terms which the pupils should learn to use, and the best method of teaching them is to place the diagrams shown on pages 181, 184, 185, on the blackboard, and leave them there for a time.

Since mushrooms are especially good subjects for water-color and pencil studies, it would add much to the interest of the work if each pupil, or the school as a whole, should make a portfolio of sketches of all the species found. With each drawing there should be made on a supplementary sheet a spore-print of the species. White paper should be covered very thinly with white of egg or mucilage, so as to hold fast the discharged spores when making these prints for portfolio or herbarium.

Observations—

1. Where was the mushroom found? If on the ground, was the soil wet or dry? Was it in open fields or in woods? Or was it found on rotten wood, fallen leaves, old trees or stumps, or roots? Were there many or few specimens?

2. Is the cap cone-shaped, bell-shaped, convex, plane, concave, or funnel-form? Has it a raised point at the center? How wide is it?

3. What is the color of the upper surface of the cap when young? When old? Has it any spots of different colors on it? Has it any striate markings, dots or fine grains on its surface? Is its texture smooth or scaly? Is its surface dull, or polished, or slimy? Break the cap and note the color of the juice. Is it milky?

4. Look beneath the cap. Is the under surface divided into plates like the leaves of a book, or is it porous?

5. The plates which may be compared to the leaves of a book are called gills, although they are not for the purpose of breathing, as are the gills of a fish. Are there more gills near the edge of the cap than near the stem? How does this occur? What are the colors of the gills? Are the gills the same color when young as when old? Are the lower edges of the gills sharp, blunt or saw-toothed?

6. Break off a cap and note the relation of the gills to the stem. If they do not join the stem at all they are termed "free." If they end by being joined to the stem, they are called "adnate" or "adnexed." If they extend down the stem they are called "decurrent."

7. Take a freshly opened mushroom, cut off the stem, even with the cap, and set the cap, gills down, on white paper; cover with a tumbler,

The gills on a common edible mushroom can be used as a stamp to create an interesting print.

or other dish to exclude draught; leave it for twenty-four hours and then remove the cover, lift the cap carefully and examine the paper. What color is the imprint? What is its shape? Touch it gently with a pencil and see what makes the imprint. Can you tell by the pattern where this fine dust came from? Examine the dust with a lens. This dust is made up of mushroom spores, which are not true seeds, but which do for mushrooms what seeds do for plants. How do you think the spores are scattered? Do you know that one little grain of this spore dust would start a new growth of mushrooms?

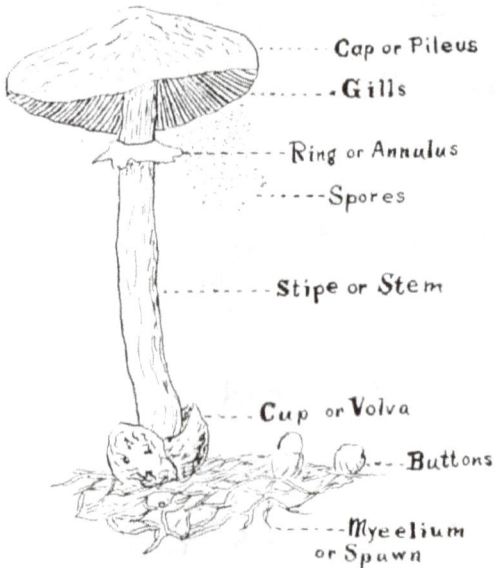

Mushroom with parts named.

8. Look at the stem.

What is its length? Its color? Is it slender or stocky? Is its surface shiny, smooth, scaly, striate or dotted? Has it a collar or ring around it

Gills free

Gills adnexed

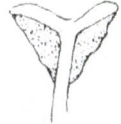

Gills decurrent

near the top? What is the appearance of this ring? Is it fastened to the stem, or will it slide up and down? Is the stem solid or hollow? Is it swollen at its base? Is its base set in a sac or cup, or is it covered with a membrane which scales off? Do you know that the most poisonous of mushrooms have the sac or the scaly covering at the base of the stem?

9. Examine with a lens the material on which the mushroom was growing; do you see any threads in it that look like mold? Find if you can what these threads do for the mushroom. If you were to go into the mushroom business what would you buy to start your beds? What is mushroom "spawn?"

10. If you can find where the common edible mushrooms grow plentifully, or if you know of any place where they are grown for the market, get some of the young mushrooms when they are not larger than a pea and others that are larger and older. These young mushrooms are called "buttons." Find by your own investigation the relation between the buttons and the threads. Can you see the gills in the button? Why? What becomes of the veil over the gills as the mushrooms grow large?

11. Do you know the difference between mushrooms and toadstools? Do you know the common edible mushroom when you see it? What characters separate this from the poisonous species? What is the "death cup," as it is called, which covers the base of the stem of the most common poisonous species?

The shape at the base of the mushroom can help you identify the type

185

Puffballs

TEACHER'S STORY

THE puffballs are always interesting to children, because of the "smoke" which issues from them in clouds when they are pressed between thumb and finger. The common species are white or creamy when young; and some of the species are warty or roughened, so that as children we called them "little lambs." They grow on the ground usually, some in wet, shady places, and others, as the giant species, in grassy

DARIO13 (CC BY-SA3.0)

Cup-shaped puffball, Calvatia cyathiformis. This edible puffball may reach 6 inches in diameter; it is found on open grassy ground in early autumn

fields in late summer. This giant puffball always excites interest, when found. It is a smoothish, white, rounded mass, apparently resting on the grass as if thrown there; when lifted it is seen that it has a connection below at its center, through its mycelium threads, which form a network in the soil. It is often a foot in diameter, and specimens four feet through have been recorded. When its meat is solid and white to the very center, it makes very good food. The skin should be pared off, the meat sliced and sprinkled with salt and pepper and fried in hot fat until browned. All the puffballs are edible, but ignorant persons might mistake the button stages of some of the poisonous mushrooms for little puffballs, and it is not well to encourage the use of small puffballs for the table.

Earth-star

A common species—"the beaker puffball"—is pear-shaped, with its small end made fast to the ground, which is permeated with its vegetative threads.

The interior of a puffball, "the meat," is made up of the threads and spores. As they ripen, the threads break up so that with the spores they make the "smoke," as can be seen if the dust is examined through a microscope. The outer wall may become dry and brittle and break open to allow the spores to escape, or one or more openings may appear in it as spore doors. The spores of puffballs were used extensively in pioneer days to stop the bleeding of wounds and especially for nosebleed.

In one genus of the puffball family, the outer coat splits off in points on maturing, like an orange peel cut lengthwise in six or seven sections but still remaining attached to the base. There is an inner coat that remains as a protection to the spores, so that these little balls are set each in a little star-shaped saucer. These star points straighten out flat or even curl under in dry weather, but when damp they lift up and again envelop the ball to a greater or less extent.

Giant puffball, Calvatia gigantea. It is not unusual to find these puffballs 10 to 20 inches in diameter. This is the largest puffball and is a great favourite among the edible varieties. In prime condition the flesh is white; it is edible as long as it remains white

LESSON

Leading thought— The puffballs are fungi that grow from the threads, or mycelium, which permeate the ground or other matter on which the puffballs grow. The puffballs are the fruiting organs, and "smoke" which issues from them is largely made up of spores, which are carried off by the wind and sown and planted.

Method— Ask the pupils to bring to school any of the globular or pear shaped fungi in the early stages when they are white, taking pains to bring them on the soil or wood on which they are growing.

Observations—

1. Where did you find the puffball? On what was it growing? Were there many growing in company? Remove the puffball, and examine the place where it stood with a lens to find the matted and crisscrossed fungus threads.

2. What is the size and shape of the puffball? Is its surface smooth or warty? What is its color inside and outside?

3. Have you ever found the giant puffball, which may become four inches to four feet through? Where was it growing? Have you ever eaten this puffball sliced and fried? Do you know by the looks of the meat when it is fit to eat?

4. If the puffball is ripe, what is its color outside and in? What is the color of its "smoke"? Does the smoke come out through the broken covering of the puffball, or are there one or more special openings to allow it to escape?

5. Puff some of the "smoke" on white paper and examine it with a lens. What do you think this dust is? Of what use is it to the puffball?

6. Have you ever found what are called earth-stars, which look like little puffballs set in star-shaped cups? If you find these note the following things:

a. Of what is the star-shaped base made? Was it always there?

b. Let this star saucer become very dry; how does it act?

c. Wet it; and how does it behave then?

d. Where and how does the spore dust escape from the earth-stars?

7. For what medicinal purpose is the "smoke" of the puffball sometimes used?

H. Krisp (cc by 3.0)

The mature spores escape through the openings you can see on top of the puffballs.

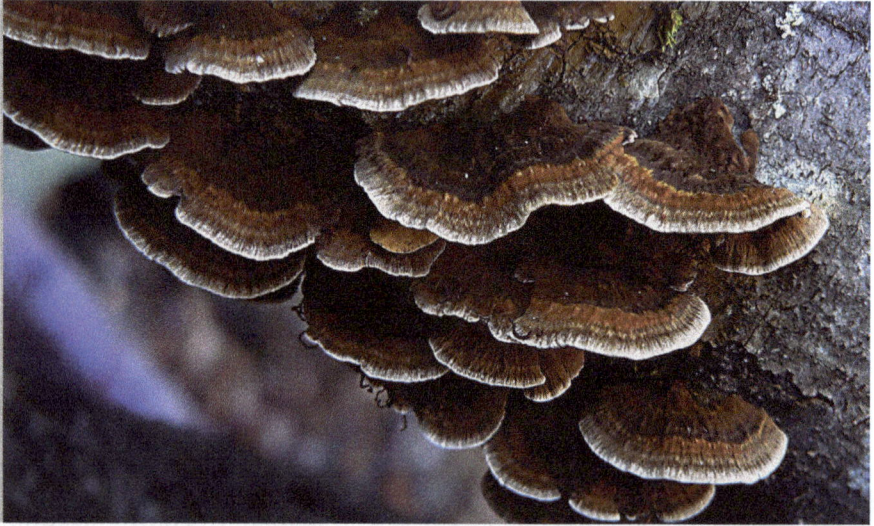

The Bracket Fungi

THERE are some naturalists who think that one kind of life is as good as another and therefore call all things good. Perhaps this is the only true attitude for the nature lover. To such the bracket-like fungi which appear upon the sides of our forest and shade trees are simply an additional beauty, a bountiful ornamentation. But some of us have become special pleaders in our attitude toward life, and those of us who have come to feel the grandeur of tree life can but look with sorrow upon these fungus outgrowths, for they mean that the doom of the tree is sealed.

There are many species of bracket fungi. Three of these are very common. The gray bracket, gray above and with creamy surface below (*Polyporous applanatus*) is a favorite for amateur etchers, who with a sharp point make interesting sketches upon this naturally prepared plate; this species often grows to great size and is frequently very old. Another species (*P. lucidus*) is in color a beautiful mahogany, or coral-red above and has a peculiar stem from which it depends; the stem and upper surface are polished as if burnished and the lower surface is yellowish white. Another species (*P. sulphurens*) is sulphur yellow

190

A bracket fungus, Polyporus versicolor. *This is a common form of Polyporus found on dead wood. When wet this fungus is flexible but when dry it is woody, and almost brittle*

above and below; usually many of these yellow brackets are grouped together, their fan-shaped caps overlapping. Many of the shelf fungi live only on dead wood, and those are an aid in reducing dead branches and stumps until they crumble and become again a part of the soil. However, several of the species attack living trees and do great damage. They can gain access to the living tree only through an injured place in the bark, a break caused perhaps by the wind, by a bruise from a falling tree, or more often from the hack of the careless wood-chopper; often they gain entrance through an unhealed knot-hole. To one who understands trees and loves them, their patient striving to heal these wounds inflicted by forces they cannot withstand is truly pathetic. After the wound is made and before the healing is accomplished, the wind may sift into the wound the almost omnipresent spores of these fungi and the work of destruction begins. From the spores grows the mycelium, the fungus threads which push into the heart of the wood getting nourishment from it as they go. When we see wood thus diseased we say that it is rotting, but rotting merely means the yielding up of the body substance of the tree to these voracious fungus threads. They push in radially and then grow upward and downward, weakening the tree where it most needs strength to withstand the onslaught of the wind. Later these parasitic threads

Oyster mushroom, Pleurotus ostreatus

may reach the cambium layer, the living ring of the tree trunk, and kill the tree entirely; but many a tree has lived long with the fungus attacking its heartwood. A bracket fungus found by Professor Atkinson was eighty years old; however, this may have shortened the life of the tree a century or more.

After these fungus threads are thoroughly established in the tree, they again seek a wound in the protecting bark where they may push out and build the fruiting organ, which we call the bracket. This may be at the same place where the fatal entry was made, or it may be far from it. The bracket is at first very small and is composed of a layer of honeycomb cells, closed and hard above and opening below—cells so small that we can see the cell openings only with a lens. These cells are not hexagonal like the honeycomb, but are tubes packed together. Spores are developed in each tube. Next year another layer of cells grows beneath this first bracket and extends out beyond it; each year it is thus added to, making it thicker and marking its upper surface with concentric rings around the point of attachment. The creamy surface of the great bracket fungus on which etchings are made, is composed of a layer of these minute spore-bearing tubes. Not all bracket fungi show their age by these annual growths, for some species form new shelves every year, which decay after the spores are ripened and shed.

When once the mycelium of such fungus becomes established, the tree is doomed and its lumber made worthless even though, as sometimes happens, the tree heals its wounds so that the fungus is imprisoned and can never send out fruiting brackets. Thus it is most important to teach the pupils how to protect trees from the attacks of these enemies, which are devastating our forests and which sometimes at-tack our orchards and shade trees.

This woody type of pore fungi, Gandoderma, *usually found growing on old wood has a brittle polished crust*

As soon as a tree is bruised, the wound should be painted or covered with a coat of tar. If the wind breaks a branch, the splinters left hanging should be sawed off, leaving a smooth stump, and this be painted. While ordinary paint if renewed each year will suffice, experiment has shown that the coat of tar is better and should be used.

Especially should teachers impress on pupils the harm done by careless hacking with axe or hatchet. We shall do an invaluable service in the protection of our forests, if we teach the rising generation the respectful treatment of trees—which is due living organisms whose span of life may cover centuries.

LESSON

Leading thought— The fungi which we see growing shelflike from trees, are deadly enemies to the trees. Their spores germinate and penetrate at some open wound and the growing fungus weakens the wood.

Method— It is desirable that a tree on which shelf fungus grows should be studied by the class, for this is a lesson on the care of trees. After this lesson the fungus itself may be studied at leisure in the schoolroom.

Observations—

1. On what kind of a tree is the bracket fungus growing? Is it alive or dead? If living, does it look vigorous or is it decaying?

Edible boletus, Botelus edulis. *This is a common plant in woods and open places during July and August. It has tubes instead of gills below the cap. The spores are developed within the tubes, as in the bracket fungi.*

2. Is the fungus bracket growing against the side of the tree, or does it stand out on a stem?

3. Look at the place where the bracket joined the tree. Does it seem to be a part of the wood?

4. What color is the fungus on its upper surface? How large is it? How thick near the tree? How thick at the edge? Can you detect concentric layers or rings? If it is the large species used for etching, cut down through it with a knife or hatchet and count the layers; this should show its age.

5. Look at the lower surface. How does it appear to the naked eye? If you scratch it with a pin or knife does the bruise show? Examine the surface with a lens and describe what you see. Cut or break the fungus and note that each of these holes is an opening to a little tube. In each of these tubes spores are borne.

6. Have you ever seen toadstools that, instead of having the leaflike gills, have beneath the cap a porous surface like a little honeycomb or like the under side of the shelf fungi?

7. How many kinds of shelf fungi can you find? Which of them is on living trees, and which on stumps or dead wood?

8. If the fungus is on a living tree, then the tree is ruined, for the fungus threads have worked through it and weakened it so that it will break easily and is of no use as lumber. There must have been an open wound in the tree where the fungus entered; see whether you can find this wound. There must also have been a wound where the shelf grew out; see whether you can detect it. If the tree should heal all its wounds after the fungus entered, what would become of the fungus?

9. What does the shelf fungus feed on? What part of it corresponds to the roots and leaves of other plants? What part may be compared to the flowering and fruiting parts of plants?

10. What treatment must we give trees to keep them free from this enemy?

Hedgehog Fungi

LESSON

THERE is something mysterious about all fungi, but perhaps none of these wonderful organisms so strangely impresses the observer as the fountainlike masses of creamy white or the branching white coral that we see growing on a dead tree trunk. The writer remembers as a child that the finding of these woodland treasures made her feel as if she were in the presence of the supernatural, as if she had discovered a fairy grotto or a kobold cave. The prosaic name of hedgehog fungi has been applied to these exquisite growths. Their life story is simple enough. The spores falling upon dead wood start threads which ramify within it and feed on its substance, until strong enough to send out a fruiting organ. This consists of a stem, dividing into ascending branches; from these branches, depending like the stalactites in a cave, are masses of drooping spines, the surface of each bearing the spores. And it is so natural for these spines to hang earthward that they are invariably so placed when the tree is in the position in which

Close up of the spines

they grew. There is one species called the "satyr's beard," sometimes found on living trees, which is a mere bunch of downward-hanging spines; the corallike species is called *Hydnum coraloides*, and the one that looks like an exquisite white frozen fountain, and may be seen in late summer or early autumn growing from dead limbs or branches, is the bear's head fungus; it is often eight inches across.

Observations—

1. These fungi come from a stem which extends into the wood.

2. This stem divides into many branchlets.

3. From these branchlets there hang long fleshy fringes like miniature icicles.

4. These fringes always hang downward when the fungus is in natural position.

5. These fringes bear the spores.

Bears head fungus growing on a log. Note the bracket mushroom also growing in the background

The Scarlet Saucer

LESSON

THE heart of the child, searching the woods for hepaticas—woods where snow banks still hold their ground on north slopes—is filled with delight at finding these exquisite saucerlike fungi. They are more often found on fallen rotting branches which are more or less buried in leaves, and there are likely to be several of different sizes on the same stick. When they grow unhindered and while they are young, they are very perfectly saucer-shaped and range from the size of a pea to an inch or two across. But the larger they are the more likely are they to be distorted, either by environment or by the bulging of rapid growth. The under side of the saucer is beautifully fleshlike in color and feeling and is attached at the middle to the stick. The inside of the saucer is the most exquisite scarlet shading to crimson. This crimson lining bears the spores in little sacs all over its surface.

Observations—

1. Where did you find the fungus?

2. What is the shape of the saucer? How large is it? Is it regular and beautiful or irregular and distorted?

3. What is the color inside?

4. What is the color outside?

5. Turn the one you bring in bottom side up—that is, scarlet side down—on a piece of white paper, and see whether you can get a spore harvest.

The Morels

An edible morel, Morchella esculenta

IN May or June in open, damp places, as orchards or the moist fence corners of meadows, the morels may be found. This mushroom family contains no member that is poisonous, and the members are very unlike any other family in appearance. They are very pretty with their creamy white, thick, swollen stems and a cap more or less conical, made up of the deep-celled meshes of an unequal network. The outside edges of the network are yellowish or brownish when the morel is young and edible, but later turn dark as the spores develop. In some species the stems are comparatively smooth and in others their surface is more or less wrinkled. The spores are borne in the depressions of the network. These mushrooms should not be eaten after the cells change from creamy white to brownish.

Observations—

1. Where did you find the morels?

2. Describe the stem. Is it solid or hollow? Is it smooth or rough?

3. What is the shape of the cap? How does it look? What color is the outer edge of the network? What is the color within the meshes?

4. Take one of these fungi, lay it on a sheet of white paper, and note the color of the spores.

The Stink-
horns

LESSON

TO give a nature-study lesson on the stinkhorn is quite out of the question, for the odor of these strange growths is so nauseating that even to come near to one of them in the garden is a disagreeable experience. The reason for mentioning them at all is because of the impression made by them that most mushrooms are ill smelling, which is a slander.

It is a pity that these fungi are so offensive that we do not care to come near enough to them to admire them, for they are most interesting in appearance. The scientific name of our commonest genus when translated means "the net bearers," and it is a most appropriate name. The stout, white stem is composed of network without and within. The outer covering of the stem seems to tear loose from the lower portion as the stem elongates, and is lifted so that it hangs as a veil around the bottom of the bell-shaped cap, which is always covered with a pitted network. The mycelium, or spawn, of the stinkhorn consists of strands which push their way through the ground or through the decaying vegetable matter on which they feed. On these strands are produced the stinkhorns, which at first look like eggs; but later the top of the egg is broken, and the strange horn-shaped fungus pushes up through it. The spores are borne in the chambers of the cap, and when ripe the substance of these chambers dissolves into a thick liquid in which the spores float. The flies are attracted by the fetid odor and come to feast upon these fungi and to lay their eggs within them, and incidentally they carry the spores away on their brushy feet, and thus help to spread the species.

Clathrus archeri, *commonly known as octopus stinkhorn, or devil's fingers, is a fungus indigenous to Australia, including Tasmania, and New Zealand, and an introduced species in Europe, North America and Asia.*

The fruiting body of a stinkhorn fungus emerges from the ground as an egg-like structure. It then splits open, revealing a stalk with a number of coloured arms. This species, Anthurus archeri, is growing in a clump of moss in native forest. Stinkhorn fungi produce a smelly mucus mass full of spores at the base of their arms. Flies feed on the stinking mucus and in so doing help to spread the spores.

Mold is an unusual fungus that can be seen in detail only under a microscope, but their overgrown colonies are visible to the naked eye.

Molds

TEACHER'S STORY

IT is lucky for our peace of mind that our eyes are not provided with microscopic lenses, for then we should know that the dust, which seems to foregather upon our furniture from nowhere, is composed of all sorts of germs, many of them of the deadly kind. The spores of mold are very minute objects, the spore-cases being the little white globes, not larger than the head of a small pin which we see upon mold, yet each of these spore-cases breaks and lets out into the world thousands of spores, each one ready and anxious to start a growth of mold and perfectly able to do it under the right conditions; almost any substance which we use for food, if placed in a damp and rather dark place, will prove a favorable situation for the development of the spore which swells, bursts its wall and sends out a short thread. This gains nourishment, grows longer and branches, sending out many threads, some of which go down into the nutritive material and are called the mycelium. While these threads, in a way, act like roots, they are not true roots. Presently the tip ends of the threads, which are spread out in the air above the bread or other material, begin to enlarge, forming little globules; the substance (protoplasm) within them breaks up into little round bodies, and each develops a cell wall and thus becomes a

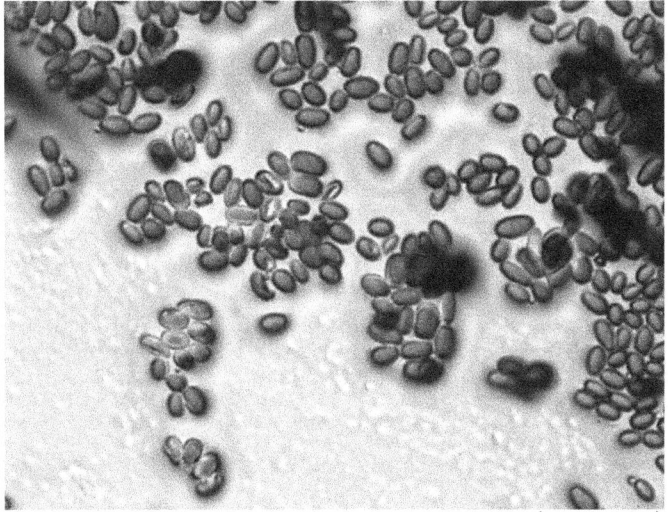

Spores from green mold growing on an orange

spore. When these are unripe they are white but later, they become almost black. In the blue mold the spores are borne in clusters of chains, and resemble tiny tassels instead of growing within little globular sacs.

Molds, mildews, blights, rusts and smuts are all flowerless plants and, with the mushrooms, belong to the great group of fungi. Molds and mildews will grow upon almost any organic substance, if the right conditions of moisture are present, and the temperature is not too cold.

Molds of several kinds may appear upon the bread used in the experiments for this lesson. Those most likely to appear are the bread mold—consisting of long, white threads tipped with white, globular spore-cases, and the green cheese-mold—which looks like thick patches of blue-green powder. Two others may appear, one a smaller white mold with smaller spore-cases, and a black mold. However, the bread mold is the one most desirable for this lesson, because of its comparatively large size. When examined with a lens, it is a most exquisite plant. The long threads are fringed at the sides, and they pass over and through each other, making a web fit for fairies—a web all beset with the spore-cases, like fairy pearls. However, as the spores ripen, these spore-cases turn black, and after a time so many of them

Several species of mold growing on a loaf of bread

are developed and ripened that the whole mass of mold is black. The time required for the development of mold varies with the temperature. For two or three days nothing may seem to be happening upon the moist bread; then a queer, soft whiteness appears in patches. In a few hours or perhaps during the night, these white patches send up white fuzz which is soon dotted with tiny pearl-like spore-cases. At first there is no odor when the glass is lifted from the saucer, but after the spores ripen, the odor is quite disagreeable.

The special point to teach the children in this lesson is that dryness and sunlight are unfavorable to the development of mold; and it might be well to take one of the luxuriant growths of mold developed in the dark, uncover it and place it in the sunlight, and see how soon it withers. The lesson should also impress upon them that dust is composed, in part, of living germs waiting for a chance to grow.

LESSON

Leading thought— The spores of mold are everywhere and help to make what we call dust. These spores will grow on any substance which gives them nourishment, if the temperature is warm, the air moist and the sunlight is excluded.

Method— Take bread in slices two inches square, and also the juice of apple sauce or other stewed fruit. Have each pupil, or the one who

Mold growing on a bunch of grapes

does the work for the class, provided with tumblers and saucers. Use four pieces of bread cut in about two-inch squares, each placed on a saucer; moisten two and leave the other two dry. With a feather or the finger take some dust from the woodwork of the room or the furniture and with it lightly touch each piece of bread. Cover each with a tumbler. Set one of the moistened pieces in a warm, dark place and the other in a dry, sunny place. Place a dry piece in similar situations. Let the pupils examine these every two or three days.

Put fruit juice in a saucer, scatter a little dust over it and set it in a warm, dark place. Take some of the same, do not scatter any dust upon it, cover it safely with a tumbler and put it in the same place as the other. A lens is necessary for this lesson, and it is much more interesting for the pupils if they can see the mold under a microscope with a three-fourths objective.

Observations—

1. When does the mold begin to appear? Which piece of bread showed it first? Describe the first changes you noticed. What is the color of the mold at first? Is there any odor to it?

2. At what date did the little branching mold-threads with round dots appear? Is there an odor when these appear? What are the colors of the dots, or spore-cases, at first? When do these begin to change color? How does the bread smell then? What caused the musty odor?

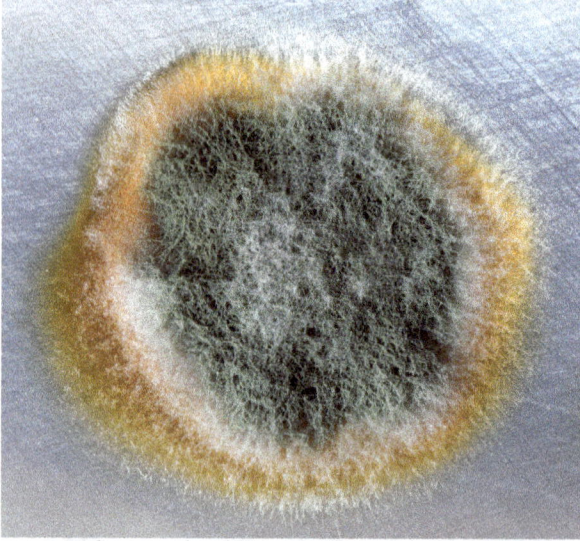
A close up of mold growing from a drop of beer

3. Did the mold fail to appear on any of the pieces of bread? If so, where were these placed? Were they moist? Were they exposed to the sunlight?

4. Did more than one kind of mold appear on the bread? If so, how do you know that they are different kinds? Are there any pink or yellow patches on the bread? If so, these are made by bacteria and not by mold.

5. From the results of the experiments, describe in what temperature mold grows best. In what conditions of dryness or moisture? Does it flourish in the sunlight or in the dark?

6. Where does the mold come from? What harm does it do? What should we do to prevent the growth of mold? Name all of the things on which you have seen mold or mildew growing.

7. Examine the mold through a microscope or a lens. Describe the threads. Describe the little round spore-cases. Look at some of the threads that have grown down into the fruit juice. Are they like the ones which grow in the air?

8. If you have a microscope cut a bit of the mold off, place it in a drop of water on a glass slide, put on a cover-glass. Examine it with a three-fourths objective, and describe the spores and spore-cases.

Bacteria

THE yellow, pink or purple spots developed upon the moist and moldy bread are caused by bacteria and yeast. Bacteria are one-celled organisms now classed as plants; they are the smallest known living beings, and can only be seen through a high power microscope.

Bacteria grow almost everywhere—in the soil, on all foods and fruits, in the water of ponds, streams and wells, in the mouths and stomachs of human beings, and in fact in almost all possible places, and occur in the air. Most of them are harmless, some of them are useful, and some produce disease in both plants and animals, including man.

What bacteria do would require many large volumes to enumerate. Some of them develop colors or pigments; some produce

Green sulfur bacteria in a Winogradsky column

gases, often ill-smelling; some are phosphorescent; some take nitrogen from the air and fix it in the soil; some produce putrefaction; and some produce disease. Nearly all of the "catching diseases" are produced by bacteria. Diphtheria, scarlet fever, typhoid fever, consumption, influenza, grippe, colds, cholera, lockjaw, leprosy, blood poisoning and many other diseases are the result of bacteria. On the other hand, many of the bacteria are beneficial to man. Some forms ripen

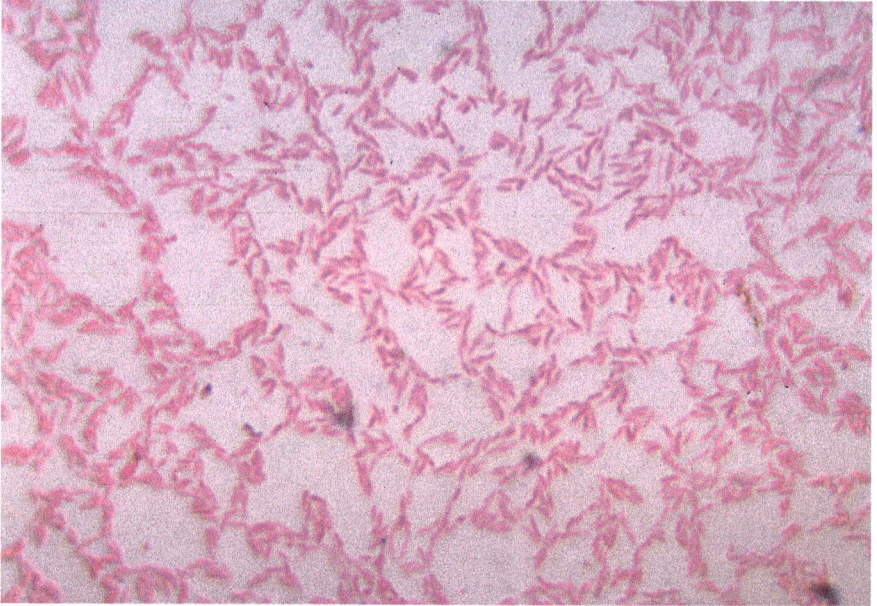

A close up of Bacteroides biacutis, *found in the gastrointestinal tract and cultured in blood agar medium for 48 hours.*

the cream before churning, others give flavor to butter; while some are an absolute necessity in making cheese. The making of cider into vinegar is the work of bacteria; some clear the pollution from ponds and streams; some help to decompose the dead bodies of animals, so that they return to the dust whence they came.

We have in our blood little cells whose business it is to destroy the harmful bacteria which get into the blood. These little fighting cells move everywhere with our blood, and if we keep healthy and vigorous by right living, right food and exercise, these cells may prove strong enough to kill the disease germs before they harm us. Direct sunlight also kills some of the bacteria. Seven or eight minutes exposure to bright sunlight is said to kill the germs of tuberculosis. Exposure to the air is also a help in subduing disease germs. Bichloride of mercury, carbolic acid, formaldehyde and burning sulphur also kill germs, and may be applied to clothing or to rooms in which patients suffering from these germ diseases have been. We can do much to protect ourselves from harmful bacteria by being very clean in our persons and in our homes, by bathing frequently and washing our hands with soap

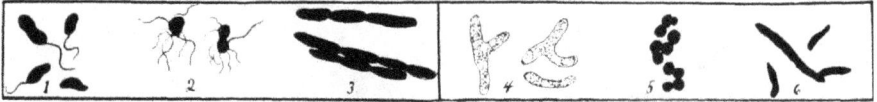

1, A bacillus which causes cholera.
2, A bacillus which causes typhoid.
3, A bacillus found in sewage.
All these are much enlarged

4, Bacteria from tubercle on white sweet
clover, much enlarged.
5 and 6, Bacteria of lactic acid ferments in
ripening of cheese, much enlarged

often. We should eat only pure and freshly cooked food, we should get plenty of sleep and admit the sunlight to our homes; we should spend all the time possible in the open air and be careful to drink pure water. If we are not sure that the water is pure, it should be boiled for twenty minutes and then cooled for drinking.

In Experiment A the milk vials and the corks are all boiled, so that we may be sure that no other bacteria than the ones we chose are present, since boiling kills these germs. As soon as the milk becomes discolored we know that it is full of bacteria.

Experiment B shows that bacteria can be transplanted to gelatin, which is a material favorable for its growth. But the point of this experiment is to show the child that a soiled finger will have upon it germs which, by growing, cloud the gelatin. They should thus learn the value of washing their hands often or of keeping their fingers out of their mouths.

Experiment C shows the way the destructive bacteria attack the potato. The discolored spots show where the decay begins, and the odor is suggestive of decay. If a potato thus attacked is put in the bright sunlight the bacteria are destroyed, and this should enforce the moral of the value of sunshine.

References— *The Story of the Bacteria*; Dust and its Dangers, M. T. Prudden, Putnam's. *Bacteria in Relation to Country Life*, Lipman.

LESSON

Leading thought— Bacteria are such small plants that we cannot see them without the aid of a microscope, but they can be planted and will grow. The object of this lesson is to enforce cleanliness.

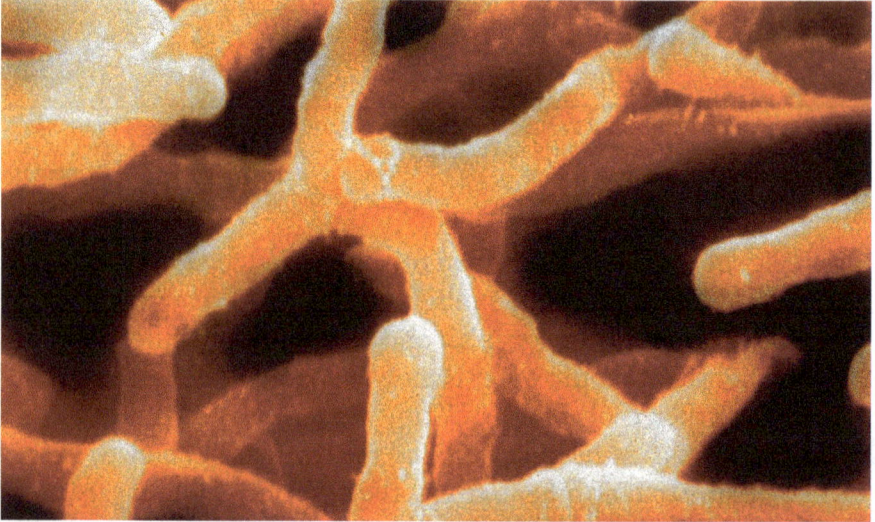

A close up of Actinobacteria. These break down organic matter so that the molecules can be reused by plants

Method—

Experiment A— The bread used for the mold experiment is likely to develop spots of yellow, red or purple upon it, and cultures from these spots may be used in this lesson as follows: Take some vials, boil them and their corks, and nearly fill them with milk that has been boiled. Take the head of a pin or hairpin, sterilize the point by holding in a flame, let it cool, touch one of the yellow spots on the bread with the point, being careful to touch nothing else, and thrust the point with the bacteria on it into the milk; then cork the vials.

Experiment B— Prepare gelatin as for the table but do not sweeten. Pour some of this gelatin on clean plates or saucers. After it has cooled let one of the children touch lightly the gelatin in one saucer for a few seconds with his soiled finger. Note the place. Ask him to wash his hands thoroughly with soap and then apply a finger to the surface of the gelatin in the other plate. Cover both plates to keep out the dust and leave them for two or three days in a dark place. The plates touched by the soiled finger will show a clouded growth in the gelatin; the other plate will show a few irregular, scattered growths or none.

Experiment C— Take a slice of boiled potato, place in a saucer, leave it uncovered for a time or blow dust upon it, label with date, then cov-

210

er with a tumbler to keep from drying and place in a cool, somewhat dark place.

The pupils should examine all these cultures every day and make the following notes:

Experiment A— How soon did you observe a change in the color of the milk? How can you tell when the milk is full of the bacteria? How do you know that the bacteria in the milk was transplanted by the pin?

Experiment B— Can you see that the gelatin is becoming clouded where the soiled finger touched it? This is a growth of the bacteria which were on the soiled finger.

Experiment C— What change has taken place in the appearance of the slice of potato? Are there any spots growing upon it? What is the odor? What makes the spots? Describe the shape of the spots. The color. Are any of them pimple-shaped? Make a drawing of the slice of potato showing the bacteria spots. What are the bacteria doing to the potato? Take a part of the slice of potato with the bacteria spots upon it, and put it in the sunshine. What happens? Compare this with the part kept in the dark.

After this lesson the children should be asked the following questions.

1. Why should the hands always be washed before eating?

2. Why should the finger nails be kept clean?

3. Why should we never bite the finger nails nor put the fingers in the mouth?

4. Why should we never put coins in the mouth?

5. Why should wounds be carefully cleansed and dressed at once?

6. Why should clothing, furniture and the house be kept free from dust?

7. Why should sweeping be done as far as possible without raising dust?

8. Why are hardwood floors more healthful than carpets?

9. Why is a damp cloth better than a feather duster for removing dust?

10. Why should the prohibition against spitting in public places be strictly enforced?

11. Why should the dishes, clothes and other articles used by sick

persons be kept distinctly separate from those used by well members of the family?

12. Why should food not be exposed for sale on the street?

13. Why, during an epidemic, should water be boiled before drinking?

"This habit of looking first at what we call the beauty of objects is closely associated with the old conceit that everything is made to please man: man is only demanding his own. It is true that everything is man's because he may use it or enjoy it, but not because it was designed and 'made' for 'him' in the beginning. This notion that all things were made for man's special pleasure is colossal self-assurance. It has none of the humility of the psalmist, who exclaimed, 'What is man, that thou art mindful of him?'

"'What were these things made for, then?' asked my friend. Just for themselves! Each thing lives for itself and its kind, and to live is worth the effort of living for man or bug. But there are more homely reasons for believing that things were not made for man alone. There was logic in the farmer's retort to the good man who told him that roses were made to make man happy. 'No, they wa'n't', said the farmer, 'or they wouldn't a had prickers.' A teacher asked me what snakes are 'good for.' Of course there is but one answer: they are good to be snakes."

—"The Nature Study Idea," L. H. Bailey.

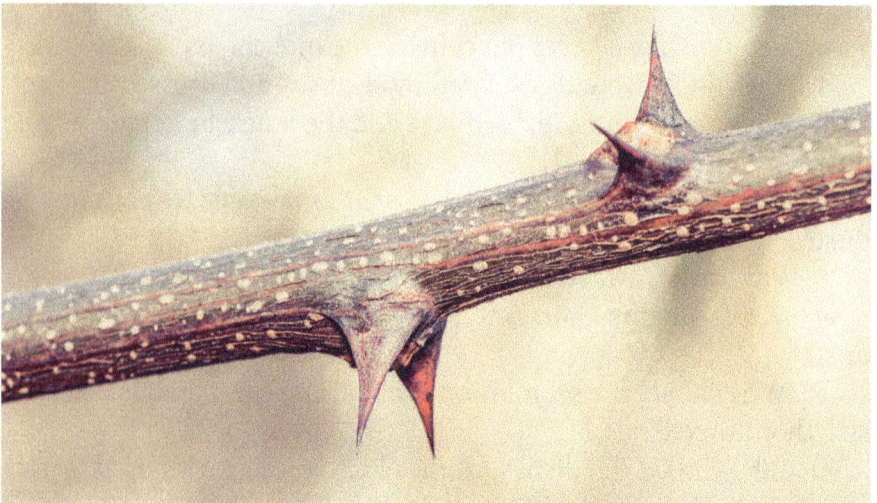